I0529326

Pandemonium Upon Pandemic

Signs Of End Of The Age

SAMUEL DAVIS KIOKO

Copyright © 2024 by Samuel Davis Kioko

All rights reserved. No parts of this book may be used or reproduced by any means, graphic, electronic, and mechanical, including photocopying, recording, taping, or by any information storage retrieval system, without the written permission of the publisher except in the case of brief quotations embodied in critical articles and reviews.

ISBN: 978-1-963565-94-2 (Paperback)
ISBN: 978-1-963565-93-5 (Ebook)

Library of Congress Control Number:
2024909301

Printed in the United States of America

Published by:

Samuel Davis Kioko
samdkioko@kiowanezus.com;
godsimage54@mail.com

Preface

Coming to you in the modality of this book means another opportunity for me of preaching the gospel standing on the word, standing in the watchman's office and doing everything within my power to bring a relative, interpretive and prophetic word to God's people.

Right now, the nation that I live in, the United States of America there has been turmoil, yet I believe God is up to something magnificent in the earth and in His church. I also believe we need to understand the times and know what to do like the sons of Issachar Tola, Puvah, Job, and Shimron who had an understanding of the times, to know what Israel ought to do, and all their brethren were at their command. Now is not the time to shy away and duck our heads and put them in the sand but pay attention to the things that are happening. Now, is the time to declare the word of God with clarity, precision, and lift our voices and believe God for healing of nations of the earth, discords, and divide. I believe supernatural transformation is already on the way. Jesus cannot come for a church that is so divided and prejudiced against one another and without love for one another. According to Ephesians 5:25-27, Jesus is coming for church that He has loved and gave Himself for her. (*25 Husbands, love your wives, just as Christ also loved the church and gave Himself for her; 26 that He might sanctify and cleanse her with the washing of water by the word, [27] that He might present her to Himself a glorious church, not having spot or wrinkle or any such thing, but that she should be holy and without blemish).*

Prayer

Father, in the name of Jesus thank You for these moments. Thank You for this time. Thank You for allowing us to be a voice in this moment to declare Your word to Your people and nations of the earth. We decree this time is a great time of revelation and transformation in the name of Jesus.

Introduction

The destination of the kingdom children is the world not the church. The church is where kingdom children go and get trained so they can take territory in the world. When the kingdom of God begins to manifest in the earth, I would like you to see what is going to happen because it is not going to look like the church as you have known it. I pray you are ready to learn from the word of God and get into some deep truths as it relates to the time we are in and the time that is coming. As you read this book you are going to encounter dynamic truths and you will be getting into a powerful emersion in the word of God.

I was impressed to write this book as Covid-19 began to sweep across the globe and after a pandemonium that rocked the core foundations of the United States of America. These are signs of the end of the age and the children of the kingdom should know they are to have an understanding of this time and know what the nations must do during and after the times of pandemonium upon pandemic sheltering. The children of the kingdom are to have an understanding of this time and know what and who is coming upon the earth. People are wondering what is going on! Whether they know it or not they are looking at the signs of the end of time, the things that are happening, sonship in the political and economic realm, and are wondering what is going on! The good news is the word of God tells us what is happening right now. The prophets have foretold of these times. These are not times to be afraid or frightened, but they are times to be knowledgeable, sober, and to be informed. The bible declares in the reign of King David, there was a group of men from the tribe of Issachar who had an understanding of the time they lived and knew what Israel (the people of God) should be doing. As you read this book you will gain an understanding of the times you are living in and know beyond a shadow of a doubt that you as a new creation in Christ Jesus, that as new covenant believer, that you as a man or woman of God in these end times should be doing and should be looking for and should be expecting. The bible states that those who exercise faith in the word and are mature in the word, get strong meat, they do not get milk. Whichever level of a believer you are you are going to be informed and instructed. If you are mature in the word of God, there are some dots in there that will be connected for you. The Spirit of wisdom and revelation of the knowledge of God is going to begin to overtake you. Your eyes are going to be enlightened and start seeing things from God's perspective. You are going to know regardless of who you are not only what time it is, but what you should be doing. I encourage you to stay engaged in reading so you can understand your responsibility in the times of the end of age on the earth. The knowledge you are going acquire is going to be invaluable to you in these days of uncertainty.

Chapter 1

During and After Times of Pandemic Sheltering

I am not an all-time prophet nor son of a prophet perse, but I do have a prophet's name though, Samuel Davis Kioko. I cannot tell you everything God is going to do during this time of sheltering but as a son of God filled with His Holy Spirit and on a mission of connecting people with the power of God and like any other son of God I have the ability to understand the times to know what I and the children God has given to me ought to do during and after the times of a pandemonium upon a pandemic and sheltering based on the scriptures and what God has done in the past during and after times of sheltering.

Once you review the truth of history as I have described below, I believe you too will know what God is going to do this time.

God sheltered Noah and his family for one year in the Ark until Noah emerged to become the father of the nations of the earth.

God sheltered Jacob in the home of his uncle, Laban when he needed to escape the wrath of Esau, his brother and twenty years later Jacob emerged with a new family, wealth, and a new identity. He became Israel the new name for God's chosen people.

God sheltered Joseph from his seventeenth

year to his thirtieth, but his slavery and prison became the school where God prepared him for greatness.

God sheltered Moses in a remote desert for forty years, but Moses came forth to liberate the Jewish people from Egypt.

God sheltered Naomi in the barren land of Moab until she nearly became bitter. But she and her daughter's in-law, Ruth travelled to Bethlehem to participate in one of the greatest love stories of history. God sheltered David for fifteen years after he had been anointed king of Israel. When David finally assumed the throne, he was a man after God's own heart, and he gave us many of the Psalms. God sheltered Elijah by the Brook Cherith and after the sheltering, he stood alone against the prophet of Baal on Mount Carmel.

God sheltered Jonah for three days and three nights in the belly of the whale. When the sheltering was over Jonah went to Nineveh and preached history's greatest revival.

God sheltered Daniel for seventy years in Babylon where he wrote his Old Testament book bearing his name outlining the future of God's dealings with His people.

God sheltered Esther while in the palace of Persian king and she saved her people from destruction.

God sheltered the disciples in the upper room for ten days until the Holy
Spirit descended in a dramatic fashion to form the church.

God sheltered apostle Paul in the Arabic desert for three years and when he came back, he turned the world upside down. God later sheltered the apostle Paul in a Roman prison and by the time the apostle was released he had written the epistles of Ephesians, Philippians, Colossians, and Philemon.

God sheltered the apostle John in the Island of Patmos and wrote the book of Revelation; the greatest prophetic document of all time was given us.

God sheltered the children of Israel in Egypt during the times of plagues. When there were plagues in the houses of the Egyptians there were wonders in the houses of the God's people at Goshen.

Lastly and incredibly God sheltered Jesus Christ in a tomb for three days and on the third day Jesus came forth in power to bring salvation to the whole world.

So now, I do not know all the details about what God is going to do, but what I do know is what He has done and that is what we can count on. The God who sheltered His people in the biblical days will not stop now. So come what may I am trusting in the sheltering God to be my refuge and say with Isaiah in 25:4 – *"You have been a refuge to the poor, a refuge for the needy in their distress, a shelter from the storm and shade from the heat"*.

Across the United States of America on May 31, 2020, we awoke to a significant time of demonstration pandemonium upon the Covid-19 pandemic. Probably you are reading from another nation and at a later time. Just as we were trying to open up the country for business as usual from the Coronavirus pandemic a demonstration of pandemonium literally hit every state. It was seen erupting in television stations and has come with questions that I must give answers to as the scripture in *1 Peter 3:15 says – But sanctify the Lord God in your hearts, and always be ready to give a defense/answer to everyone who asks you a reason for the hope that is in you, with meekness and fear.*

What is this we are experiencing and how are we to respond to it as a new creation in Christ Jesus? As I prayed, listened to the Holy Spirit, and watched the news I wondered how I was going to respond to the situation at hand seeing that Justice was not rendered and yet the citizens are demanding it in the wake of the murder of a black man by a white police officer.

We are experiencing a divide among the citizens of the United States and yet on the day of Pentecost, we read about it as a time literally when the Holy Spirit was poured out in Jerusalem and the church was born and brought people together across ethnic groups and we are witnessing here in the United States one of the greatest hours of division that we have ever seen. This is a play of the enemy and only the wisdom of God, the word of God, and the prayers of God's prophetic people can make a difference. I know you may say we have prayed and continue to pray for our land. Good, we have done well, but I do not believe that prayer alone is the answer.

I believe that without prayer answers will never actually come and never actually manifest. I am certain that when in times of crisis you asses what you should do. One of the things you evaluate is what you can do that no one else can do. The thing that someone else can do is to call upon the name of the Lord and seek Him for His wisdom, direction, and answers.

The Spirit of God is being poured out in a fresh way in this hour because the adversary wants to throw out everything that God has purposed, but I am determined as a weapon of war in the hand of God will not let that happen. All across the globe especially here in the United States over the last couple of days people were beginning to celebrate the reopening for normalcy in the middle of the Covid-19 pandemic. My concern is that the United States has no idea of what it has opened itself to by this pandemonium. I believe I believe that in the hand of God, there is an answer and opportunity to bring healing, but more than healing is required here. There is an opportunity to bring hope and more than hope is required. People of God are so integral to what is happening in the earth. These times are so important that you and I stay connected in the bond of Christ.

Jesus is the Lord and there is none other than Him. If you are listening like me, you know all shall be well with the righteous. *Isaiah 3:10 – "Say to the righteous that it shall be well with them, For they shall eat the fruit of their doings"* and yet we are experiencing in the United States of America not only the ramifications of the coronavirus pandemic, but we are also experiencing a pandemonium in our cities. Many people are awakening asking what is going on in the earth. I believe God has an answer and His word grants us access not only to His mind but the fullness of His Spirit.

In this book, we share some things from the word of God that I believe are vital in having the mind of the Spirit of God.

We are grateful to God for the things he has enabled us to accomplish during the coronavirus pandemic experience as they were being received as God released in the lives of people. So, we do not have bad news to bring to you but to tell you that all things are working together for the good of those who love the Lord and are called according to His purpose. I believe it is the plan of the adversary, the wicked one at this time to steal, to kill, and to destroy.

The scripture tells us that we are not to be ignorant of the devices of Satan and it is the plan of the wicked one at this time in the United States to sow seeds of division, strife, and discords because where there is division strife and discord, the move of the Spirit of God and His purpose can be hindered. That is why it is important that the people of God are not just dialed in what is being said in the news media and what is happening around us but be dialed in hearing from God even in the presence of injustice, and incomprehensible activity. God's people need to address that and tune in to the Spirit of God.

Chapter 2

Our Connection is going to Invaluable

The scripture says in *1 Corinthians 1:10* – *"Now I plead with you, brethren, by the name of our Lord Jesus Christ, that you all speak the same thing, and that there be no divisions among you, but that you be perfectly joined together in the same mind and in the same judgment"*. I sense in my spirit that it is important to look into the word of God concerning the things that are happening in the globe now and examine what is happening in the earth, assess as a prophetic people and respond to it and not just react to the situations. As we have seen in the news media recently, we all have been impacted, horrified, perhaps angered and wept, I have. Perhaps you asked what is going on all over the globe once again and wandered, a pandemonium upon a pandemic! Here in California, we were experiencing real turmoil in the streets in response in part to (what transpired in Minneapolis St. Paul Minnesota) the murder of a black man by a white police officer here in the United States of America where we are watching from all over the globe. When we get so far down in life, we have nowhere to look but up. I have had the privilege of schooling, working in corporate America, and living with roommates in multi-neighborhoods of diverse ethnic origins and people of all walks of life and never experienced this level of prejudice. So, I have asked of the Lord and searched the scriptures for answers not only for myself, but also for my fellow mankind. I found out that the word of God has the answer to these many questions. Therefore, I will share what the word of God has to say about a pandemonium upon a pandemic.

Throughout Christendom, this is the season we are celebrating and commemorating the season of Pentecost which is the Jewish feast. This day of Pentecost is recorded in the book of Acts 2:5-12 which gives us answers. We understand what is happening around us and how we should be responding to both the coronavirus pandemic and demonstrations of pandemonium and other things that are to be occurring. We are now in a season of commemorating and celebrating the specific day of Pentecost. We should be mindful of what is around us and how to respond to it.

Acts 2:5-12 – [5] And there were dwelling in Jerusalem Jews, devout men, from every nation under heaven. [6] And when this sound occurred, the multitude came together, and were confused, because everyone heard them speak in his own language. [7] Then they were all amazed and marveled, saying to one another, "Look, are not all these who speak Galileans? [8] And how is it that we hear, each in our own [a]language in which we were born? [9] Parthians and Medes and Elamites, those dwelling in Mesopotamia, Judea and

Cappadocia, Pontus and Asia, [10] Phrygia and Pamphylia, Egypt and the parts of Libya adjoining Cyrene, visitors from Rome, both Jews and proselytes, [11] Cretans and [b]Arabs—we hear them speaking in our own tongues the wonderful works of God." [12] So they were all amazed and perplexed, saying to one another, "Whatever could this mean?"

The phrase: "From Every Nation Under Heaven" speaks volumes. Nation is the Greek word "Ethnos" from which we get our word "Ethnic". It is especially important we understand this. Jew was their religious persuasion or religious conviction and not their ethnicity. The scriptures say they were Jews from every nation or Jews from different ethnic groups under heaven.

Chapter 3

———••✦❧·⟡⟠⟡·❧✦••———

The Mind of Spirit God

We need to understand the mind of the Spirit of God and what Satan is attempting to do right now. Both in the United States and globally we are scheduled for a fresh outpouring of the Holy Spirit for renewing in the Spirit of God. Through this season the Spirit of God desires to accomplish that, but the adversary always wants to throttle and disrupt the plans of God.

Acts 2:5 articulates a particularly important point. Day of Pentecost was one of the three annual feasts in the Jewish calendar year where all Jews came to Jerusalem to celebrate. There was a pilgrimage where they used to come, and Pentecost was one of those feasts where Jews from every nation or ethnic group would come.

The day of Pentecost was going to be the day of Pentecost whether the Holy Spirit was poured or not. We in charismatic persuasion think that Pentecost occurred only once when the Holy Spirit was poured out. The people were not there because the Holy Spirit was going to be poured out, the people were going to be there anyway. It was a regular activity of Jews around this feast they celebrated.

According to Verse 6-12, Christianity is not a white man's religion. Anybody who tells you Christianity is a white man's religion has not read their bible. What God did on the day of Pentecost was that He chose this Pentecost festival, this multicultural, multiethnic gathering of people to birth the church. So, God birthed the church as a multicultural, multiethnic people, and where those people have gathered since God pours out His Spirit and commands a blessing.

Psalm 133:1-4 says - Behold, how good and how pleasant it is for brethren to dwell together in unity! ² It is like the precious oil upon the head, running down on the beard, The beard of Aaron, running down on the edge of his garments. ³ It is like the dew of Hermon, descending upon the mountains of Zion for there the LORD commanded the blessing – Life forevermore.

The Lord commands a blessing where brethren dwell together in unity across ethnic lines, the divisive lines that cultural men have created. People especially carnal Christians have been praying for years for a move of the Spirit of God to bring people together ethnically. The fact of the matter is that there is no move of the Spirit of God that is going to bring people together ethnically. It is people who will get together across ethnic lines that the move of the Spirit of God will be commanded. Wherever it happens God will pour out distinct and special blessings. That is one of the reasons why the enemy fights it. Even in this time, the enemy has raised his head again to sow strife, discords, and division in the nation of the United States of America and the nations of the earth. That is Satan's work, that is what he does and we are not ignorant of his devices. I expect natural people to respond the way they are conditioned to respond when these types of things we have seen in the last couple of months happen. But you and I in the prophetic community and as the people of God we must look past headlines, divisions, injustice, and what the world calls racism and understand the mind and the Spirit of God. Regardless the emotions you are experiencing as a result of inhumane murder please read on to understand why and how to respond to the incident. My exaltation is for new covenant, new creation believers in Christ Jesus. I do not expect the people who are not born again even to have the capacity to function and respond scripturally, spiritually, or truly. The scripture in 1 Corinthians 2:14-15 declares that *14 But the natural man does not receive the things of the Spirit of God, for they are foolishness to him; nor can he know them, because they are spiritually discerned. 15 But he who is spiritual judges all things, yet he himself is rightly judged by no one.*

The natural man cannot even know the things that you and I are supposed to know, accept, and walk in as truth. You cannot expect the agreement of carnal men be they politicians or preachers. There are many carnal preachers who have accepted religion, but denied the power of God.

2 Timothy 3:5 - having a form of godliness but denying its power. And from such people turn away!

They have accepted a form of godliness but do not live or govern themselves by the word of God. It is a dangerous thing in this hour to be following a man or woman who has a form of godliness but has not determined that the word of God is the truth. The problem in too many a church both black and white is that we have carnal preachers in pulpits who are continually inseminating their followers with religion and not with the truth. So the scripture is stating here that the natural man who does not have eternal life and whose Spirit is not born again does not receive the things of the Holy Spirit of God. The natural man will not accept God's word as truth because it is foolishness to him and cannot even know it because the things of God are spiritually discerned. The reality is that as believers in Christ Jesus, you and I have agreed and settled that the scriptures are truth. Maybe you do not know you have agreed to that! But once you are born again you come into the kingdom of God where the scriptures are truth, not what you have been educated to understand, not what natural intelligentsia or news media gives.

Jesus states in John 17:17 speaking about His people, *"sanctify them by Your truth, your word is truth".*

The word of God is truth and your and my opinions on any matter have to be conformed to the truth of the word of God. The word of God will never conform to our opinions. Because you and I have agreed as believers in Christ Jesus that the word is truth and if you are a Christian and have not agreed to that yet, you agreed to it even though you do not know you have agreed to it. It is as if you signed your name without reading all the fine print.

In the kingdom of God, we have agreed that the word of God is TRUTH, and therefore when it comes to being a covenant, new creation believers we must always conform our opinions to God's word because God's word will never conform to our opinions. This is important because when you begin to see things that are going on in this nation on what happened a month ago that a black man, George Floyd was murdered at the knee of a Caucasian white police officer and you look at that as a believer in Christ Jesus you are enraged, saddened, perhaps you desire to retaliate. I watched at that and got genuinely angry and wept. You must understand as a child of God that you have the right to be angry. Ephesians 4:26 states that "Be angry and sin not". God or Jesus, nor the Holy Spirit restricts you from anger. And if you were an African male or female in United States of America today, you either experienced anger or you are still angry.

What you need to understand is that the scriptures give you the right to be angry, but sin not. Do not let your anger cause you to what the natural man or woman would do. Let me state some practical and spiritual things. Those who have watched the clip you have questions not only in the United States of America but in the whole wide world. You must understand the world is watching the United States of America, the land of the free and home of the brave and wondering what is wrong with us in United States. People are feeling such anger and rage and wonder what is going on in the United States of America. As a part of the prophetic community the church, how do I possibly walk in love in such a situation. How does God expect me to walk in love in such a situation? How does God expect me to walk in love in such a situation? How can I possibly love my enemy? How can I love a man who is a murderer?

Matthew 5:43-44 stats that - *43 "You have heard that it was said, 'You shall love your neighbor and hate your enemy.' 44But I say to you, love your enemies, bless those who curse you, do good to those who hate you, and pray for those who spitefully use you and persecute you,*

Here is where we have to understand we cannot preach, yell, and burn one another, but we have to understand something in the situation. These scriptures teach us that wisdom is the principal thing in any circumstance and situation. We must get wisdom which is the word of God. We have to understand things from the standpoint of God. I am writing to new creation, people born again and filled with the Spirit of God. You have to get wisdom to love an enemy like this who wants to kill you. People are offended and angry. They do not want to hear preaching, praying or anybody telling them what to do, they are offended and angry too. A lot of people who are not of color, Caucasian whether they are believers or unbelievers do not understand what people of color are going through and why the murder has made people of color so angry. To my knowledge, nobody died not only in Los Angeles, but elsewhere in the world at the hands of the police at that time, but the city was on smoke. I watched riots and looting in Philadelphia, Los Angeles, Atlanta, Chicago, New York, and Minneapolis. Immediately I knew we were up to something. When you watch police, stations burning down and the police are nowhere to be found, that is another whole level of reaction. The natural response would be it is reasonable to burn the whole city down. But we will not do that but pray and then respond not react. Prayer and prayer-inspired, and Spirit-led actions is how a new creation believer must respond. When Jesus admonished His followers to turn the other chick, He was not instructing us not just to let people slap us on both sides of our faces. Jesus stated in Matthew 5:39 – *"But I tell you not to resist an evil person. But whoever slaps you on your right cheek, turn the other to him also".*

This idea of the Christian to turn the other cheek and let people just beat them up is not what Jesus was communicating. It does not mean to be taken advantage of. What people do not understand is what we saw erupt in the United States was not just a response to what happened to George Floyd. People of color have been killed at the hands of the police. We have seen it, heard about it, prayed about it, we have matched about it, legislated about it, and talked about it. However, that is not the only thing that was being responded to. The fact of the matter is connection with that event with another event that had happened in the 24-hour news cycle of another man by the name of Christian Cooper, a filmmaker in the park in New York City and there was a white woman who was walking her dog who knew she was being filmed by Mr. Cooper. She tells the man, Mr. Cooper who is filming her "I am going to call police. She calls the police and tells them there is an African American man threatening me" and when the police answer her call, she escalates her voice and begins to scream like she is under attack. These two incidents within a twenty-four-hour news cycle said something to black people and people of color in the United States. Something that is in the secret chambers of their souls and our souls we have known all along, but still not wanted or allowed ourselves to believe.

Chapter 4

——••✠•⚜•✠••——

Here It Is

It is something that in the postmodern, post-segregation, post Jim Crow (State and local laws that enforced racial segregation in the southern United States all enacted in the late 19th and 20th century), and President Obama embracing America that has not so blatantly and visibly stated. A vast majority not everybody and no condemnation to anybody, are so comfortable, certain, and assured of their privilege and impunity believing that they will be expediently exonerated in the phase of any ill that they can and will openly and in-camera disregard life in the case of George Floyd or the wellbeing in the case of Christian Cooper, a black people without any thought of punishment and assured of presumption of innocence by the current system and establishment solely on the basis of the color of their skin. This is a problem because when you have been told things are equal in the United States and dealt with this issue which we have to address in the body of Christ you imagine you have been short-changed. The issue of challenges in the country's growing ethnic diversity where you have been told things are equal, just, and righteous yet there are people with the impunity can kill, lie, and not even fear any type of presumption of guilt and they would be assured they would get away with injustice you have now set the stage for an eruption that if not properly and spiritually dealt with will burn out of control. That is what happened in these two incidents in the United States of America.

It is not that George Floyd could not breathe with a white policeman's knee on his neck. It is because it was filmed and the policeman knowing that he was being filmed had no sense of humanity, responsibility, and a relative certainty even on camera knowing nothing will happen. This woman who later apologized knows that if she says "a black man threatening" when the police come something will happen. We need to go deeper in the prophetic community and understand something when the question is asked "Why are we feeling such rage?" That is one of the reasons you are watching people of color and I am not condoning burning buildings and other things down. That is the wrong response because the bible is telling us be angry, but sin not, do not let your anger lead you to sin.

Looking at what is happening in the United States of America we must deal with the issue of ethnicity discrimination. We must deal with it from the standpoint of truth which is the word of God. The Bible speaks a lot about this issue, but the church has not lived up to it. The answer I believe is in the Word and in the Spirit and must be modeled by the people of God before anybody else will ever be able to see this again. It is also something that has to be evidenced by the church noting that Jesus is the healer, provider, and waymaker, but Jesus is a reconciler of ethnic discords, hatred, and divisions that kept men apart.

One of the reasons in the United States of America that the pestering has continued to occur is because of the issue of Ethnic hatred. Race in its current 20th century and 21st century in politics, news media, between white and black men in its current understanding and usage in America is a white man invention. I know that bluntly because you have never seen your city on fire before, you have never seen things happen in United States of America the way it has been happening. These things must be dealt with in truth. You and I as Christians, black or white have agreed that the word is truth. It is true we have something to do with it. As I have said, in the current 20th and 21st century understanding, and usage of the word "Race" is a white man invention. It is a product of the Western predominantly European, imperialistic and colonial system of subjugation. Race is not in any way, shape, or form a divine biblical or even remotely Christian concept. The mere entertaining of the seduction to debate it is an exercise in futility that is destined for failure. It cannot produce long-lasting results. Just pay attention. We have been debating it for hundreds of years and whatever happened was short-lived.

Chapter 5

Race is an Invention

The issue of race is not a matter of truth, it is an invention. According to the biblical standpoint, there is one race, humans. Within the human race, there are distinct ethnicities. This is a distinction with a difference. The whole idea of race is a Western concept, a political system affecting the world. United States of America has been the predominant political system affecting the world and that invention has infected the entire globe. I happened to be a native of another nation, they do not speak about race, but ethnic and tribal discords. The fact of the matter is that you cannot in your Declaration of Independence write and tend the words, *"We hold these truths to be self-evident, that all men are created equal, that they are endowed by their creator with certain unalienable rights that among these are life, liberty, and the pursuit of happiness,"* - (United States declaration of independence) and then enslave another man and go to bed with a good Christian conscience, unless you have first reduced that other man to be subhuman or to be another race other than you. The whole concept of race is a dehumanization of nonwhite people in the United States of America so that the good unilluminated Christian conscience could enslave a man of another color and still say "We hold these truths to be self-evident that all men were created equal" because they are not of my level. That is the historical lie that has been perpetuated in the Western world. It has been adopted by the Christian concept, but it is not biblical. Quite frankly I am appalled to hear otherwise spiritual men and fathers in the kingdom of God who are stickers for every other aspect of accuracy of the word but continue to preach a distinction in race. If you are a white or black preacher, please understand that there is no such thing as race in the kingdom of God. There is one race, the human race. I can say that because the bible states so. May I tell you who

consider yourselves to be biblical scholars, the term race is only mentioned once in the entirety of the word of God and that is in the book of Zacharia 9:6 - *"A mixed race shall settle in Ashdod, And I will cut off the pride of the Philistines."*

Here race is not being referred to a distinction in any kind of color or dehumanization. Here the word race is translated from the Hebrew word Manzea which literally means bastard, a meaning from Jewish culture of an individual who has a Jewish father and a non-Jewish mother. It is a mixed racial set of Ashdod, meaning people with Jewish fathers and non-Jewish mothers. It is not taking about a difference in color or species. That is the only time the word race is used in the scripture, and it is not a reference to color distinction.

Acts 17:26-28 states that - *[26]And He has made from one [a]blood every nation of men to dwell on all the face of the earth, and has determined their preappointed times and the boundaries of their dwellings, [27]so that they should seek the Lord, in the hope that they might grope for Him and find Him, though He is not far from each one of us; ²⁸for in Him we live and move and have our being, as also some of your own poets have said, 'For we are also His offspring.'*

God has made all men from one blood. So, it is blood that determines race not color. It is blood that determines species not color. Man is the only one of God's creations who have been ignorant enough to accept the lie that a distinction in color denotes a distinction in race. You do not do that with birds, they are the same species with different colors. You do not do that with Horses, cattle, sheep, fish etc. They are the same species with different colors. You do not do that with dogs, they are the same species with different colors. Somehow with men we have bought the unbiblical lie and wonder why this discrimination continues. When you debate a lie based on a human premise even if you win the argument, you have not gotten closer to the truth. This bible we preach from says so. How dare you get in your church and speak to people about loving other races. There is only one race, human.

Therefore, until the church accepts it and begins to preach it, we cannot expect the word to change the mind about anything. God has made from one blood all the nations of the earth. Again, the Greek word for nations is ethnos – from which we get the English word ethnic. So, all men are the same race but different ethnicities. Ethnicity is the diversity not the race. You have to understand the historical lie of the Western European imperialistic and colonialism world is that "we have reduced you to another race so that we can justifiably with Christian conscience take advantage of you. And that is indelible in the culture and until somebody digs out the historical lie and says "Here is the lie that you have perpetuated" we are destined to continue to repeat it. This troubles me when I see white Christian's brothers who are stickers for every other aspect of the word of God, but still speak about race when it comes to your brother of another skin color. I am not sure if you are a word person at all. I think you are a favorite word person. The lie is race that we are of different race because we are of different skin color. The scriptures state that God has made all nations from one blood to dwell upon the earth. Leviticus 17:11 states that the life of the flesh is the blood not the color of the skin. *"For the life of the flesh is in the blood, and I have given it to you upon the altar to make atonement for your souls; for it is the blood that makes atonement for the soul."*

God is the evidence that we are all of the same race, and species and the blood is the issue. We are making a lie when we make variations of blood and types. You can put the blood of any man into the blood of any other man of different skin color and they will live if the blood types match not the matching of the skin color. You cannot take the horse's blood and put into a man and live because that is a different race and species.

The politician cannot handle this issue because they are ignorant of what God says about race. When you debate the issue of race and seduced into the seduction of arguing race it is important to understand from a biblical standpoint that there is only one race, human. Within that one race there is a multiplicity of ethnicities. That is the diversity, the divine of the Judeo-Christian ethic is that we are ethnically distinct, but we are racially the same. Understanding that we are ethnically distinct, but we are racially the same is important for the correction of historical lies. Second, when you start to dialogue from the standpoint that we are the same race begin in unity, not division. That is where God commands blessings, the wisdom of God can be accessed, and the answers can be brought out of the anointing of the Spirit by men and women who are honest and earnestly seeking Him. *Psalm 133:3…For there, the LORD commanded the blessing- Life forevermore.*

The problem with race if you have not noticed is even if you win the argument whose premise is a lie, you have gotten closer to the Truth. Therefore, we see the kind of things that happened with George Floyd and Christian Cooper that have been happening in the United States of America throughout our time. The only difference is that everybody has a mobile telephone, there is nothing new. This kind of injustice happens all the time who you are, where you are as a man or woman of color in the United States of America and it doesn't matter how much money you have, what you drive, and where you live you are constantly confronted by this reality. Until we begin to deal with this in truth and in Spirit there are certain things that will never ever change. I appeal to all my white brothers and sisters in the Lord, pastors, preachers, leaders, and those of you who until this time have given some degree of respect and expressing concern vocalizing empathy. I know many of you, your hearts are right and pure. I sow all ethnicities including Caucasians protesting and picketing and holding "BLACK LIVES MATTER" signs. The issue that has to be addressed now is not whether "BLACK LIVES MATTER" to you, but whether "BLACK LIVES ARE EQUAL TO YOU." Dogs' lives matter, and Whale's lives matter, but given the option of saving, a dog or a whale or a black human life which one gets more of your attention? What about black people who are responding negatively? Looting, violence, doing harm to other people's property is not acceptable either. It is wrong and as believers in Christ Jesus not only should we be engaged in it we should speak out against it. No matter who does it. The fact of the matter is until this issue is dealt with in the church, we cannot expect to see anything happen in real power or transformation in the world.

Dr. Martin Luther said that "Riot is the language of the unheard" People right now feel riot is the only way to express the rage that they feel. You are a believer in Christ Jesus you may be asking the question how do I deal with this? How can I possibly love my enemy? How can I possibly walk in love in this area?

The first thing to understand is in the gospel according to author John 3:16 God says that *"For God so loved the world that He gave His only begotten Son, that whoever believes in Him should not perish but have everlasting life."* But Genesis 6:5-8 also states *"5Then the LORD saw that the wickedness of man was great in the earth, and that every intent of the thoughts of his heart was only evil continually. [6]And the LORD was sorry that He had made man on the earth, and He was grieved in His heart. [7]So the LORD said, "I will destroy man whom I have created from the face of the earth, both man and beast, creeping thing and birds of the air, for I am sorry that I have made them."[8]But Noah found grace in the eyes of the LORD.*

God looked at the wickedness of man and he did evil continually, and God repented that He had ever made man. Here is the question! How can God love the world enough to send His son for it and at the same time look at it and repent that He had ever made it. When you understand the answer to that question then you can understand how you can walk in love no matter what people do to you. You must understand that Love is not an emotion. Love is a decision you make. People ask, how can I walk in love? You can walk in love by taking love out of the realm of emotion. You may not like what you see or like the person you are dealing with, but you cannot allow that to change how you as a believer function.

When Jesus taught about loving your enemy in Matthew 5:38-48 - *[38]"You have heard that it was said, 'An eye for an eye and a tooth for a tooth.' [39]But I tell you not to resist an evil person. But whoever slaps you on your right cheek, turn the other to him also. [40]If anyone wants to sue you and take away your tunic, let him have your cloak also. [41]And whoever compels you to go one mile, go with him two. [42]Give to him who asks you, and from him who wants to borrow from you do not turn away. [43]"You have heard that it was said, 'You shall love your neighbor and hate your enemy.' 44[a] But I say to you, love your enemies, bless those who curse you, do good to those who hate you, and pray for those who spitefully use you and persecute you, 45 that you may be sons of your Father in heaven; for He makes His sun rise on the evil and on the good, and sends rain on the just and on the unjust. 46 For if you love those who love you, what reward have you? Do not even the tax collectors do the same? 47 And if you greet your [b] brethren only, what do you do more than others? Do not even the [c] tax collectors do so? 48 Therefore you shall be perfect, just as your Father in heaven is perfect.*

This is what you and I are called to. Previously I said that Jesus is not telling us to let somebody hit both sides of our face. What Jesus was saying is this: When somebody slaps you on one side of your face respond with the side that has not been hit. If someone attacks you as a new creation in Christ Jesus, as a born-again man or woman of God you have the ability to respond out of the spirit and not out of the flesh. I learned a long time ago that I have the ability by the Holy Spirit to respond out of my spirit and not out of my mind, will, emotion and attitudes - not out of my flesh. Sometimes I want to respond out of my flesh, but I choose to respond out of my spirit. That is why God gave us the Holy Spirit so there would be the Spirit of God between the stimulus and response. If you hit the natural man he will hit you back. If you curse him out, he is going to curse you out. But for the believer, if somebody hit you before you respond it goes through the Holy Spirit and you will have the ability to choose. This is what Jesus was teaching. Jesus was not telling you to be taken advantage of but He was teaching you and I how to turn the situation so you are never the victim.

Vs40 - *40If anyone wants to sue you and take away your tunic, let him have your cloak also.*

If somebody wants to sue you do not let him sue you. Give the something. Be a giver because are called and anointed. Jesus is teaching that do not let anybody get the last word on you, but you respond out of the spirit and turn the matter, so you are always the one in charge of your response, but nobody else is in charge of it. Jesus kept it real, keep it real.

Luke 17:1-3 - *Then He (Jesus) said to the disciples, "It is impossible that no offenses should come, but woe to him through whom they do come! ²It would be better for him if a millstone were hung around his neck, and he were thrown into the sea, than that he should offend one of these little ones. ³Take heed to yourselves. If your brother sins against you, rebuke him; and if he repents, forgive him.*

When you are a child of God it is impossible that you will live and not be offended. When you get offended, Jesus gives you the right at the moment to become the most important person to yourself.

Vs3 *"Take heed to yourselves"* means that the offense is directed at you and you are the one who has to manage it. I have heard it said and it bears repeating. Being angry and offended at someone who hurts you is like drinking poison and expecting somebody else to die. You have to pay attention to yourself. The word offense in its original language is the Greek word "Skandalon" in which we get the word Scandal. It literally means a trigger on a trap. Hear what Jesus is teaching. Whenever someone offends you, they are giving you a trigger on a trap and if you put your foot on it you are the one who is going to get stuck. I got news for you. Before every major elevation or promotion there is a major offense. It is the only way the adversary can keep you from what God has for you. The adversary knows he cannot stop you, kill you, keep you out, and he knows you are not going to give up. The only thing the adversary can do is to distract you with offense to trap you and keep you from where you are.

Chapter 6

————••✦·❦·✦••————

Historical Lie

I believe now is the time for us to deal with the historical lie and begin to dialogue the matter in Truth. It is time for preachers, churches, and people of God everywhere to stop ignoring this matter and start dealing with it in truth lest it be perpetuated to the future generations. I promise you because I know this by the Spirit of God that if we would come together in unity, we can come together recognizing that we are one, God will command a blessing there and wisdom will begin to flow. *Psalm 133:1-3 – "Behold, how good and how pleasant it is for brethren to dwell together in unity! ..... for there, the LORD commanded the blessing— Life forevermore".*

It is not going to happen in the church, politics, or anywhere else. Please do not let the offense trap you. God has something on the side of this for you. There is an elevation, promotion, anointing, and favor. There is a place of increase, and there is a place power on the other side for you. People say we need a message of hope and healing. No, we need more than that, a message transformation. Hope and healing happen when transformation occurs. Transformation produces hope, and manifests healing, and the only message that transforms is the message of the gospel of Jesus Christ, the kingdom of God. The key to the ethnic division is not just dialogue, it is a transformation of heart.

Whether you realize it or not the thing that made you so affected, cried, and wept was not just the color of the two men, it was the inhumanity of one man to another. It was the fact that there seemed to be no more humanity in that action. How is that possible when the spirit is dead all manner of evil can manifest? The only answer is the transformation of the soul is the beginning of change. One of the things the book of Acts teaches us is that salvation immediately does not necessarily reject bigotry. Peter, in the day of Pentecost in Acts chapter two was there preaching but in Acts chapter ten he had to have a revelation of the Spirit of God to convince him to go to an Italian man's house, a non-Jewish man's house to preach the gospel. Peter was saved and born again, but there was still bigotry in his soul because of his tradition and upbringing. It is possible to be it a person of color Christian or a Caucasian Christian and still tolerate bigotry. There is still some remnants of bigotry and tradition in your heart as a Christian. The Holy Spirit is going to weed it out. He is going to search it out. I believe for many of these are events for last days of a revelation and understanding. Ask the Lord to help you. If you are born again regardless of your ethnicity you are my brother and sister and we have got to deal with these issues beginning with the fact that in Christ Jesus we are one. If you are not a child of God reading this book you are my colleague in human endeavor.

To all my white brothers and sisters, children of God or merely colleagues in the human condition, as we attempt to dialogue in love we must finally get to the truth. I appreciate the assertion and declaration that *"Black Lives Matter"*, but the fact should have been obvious already. The question we would pose to those of other ethnicities who were protesting supporting and carrying BLM signs is *"Are Black Lives Equal to yours, to you"?*

In the United States of America "Race" in its current 20th and 21st Century understanding and usage is a white invention. A product of the western predominantly European, imperialistic, and colonial system of subjugation for capitalistic interest. It is not in any way, shape or form "a Divine, Biblical or even Remotely Christian concept". At this point I am impressed of the Holy Spirit to pray so that transformation of the soul may start now and change may manifest.

Prayer

Father in the name of Jesus, on this season when cross Christendom celebrate the outpouring of the Holy Spirit when the church was born. The season on which You, Lord took full advantage of multicultural, multiethnic gathering and poured out Your Spirit and birthed a move in the earth and it is still going on empowering Your redeemed to be more like You. I pray my Father amidst of all the pandemonium and pandemic for the family of George Floyd and all the people who have been affected and impacted by this great injustice and yes, I declare it murder. I pray in the name of Jesus for men and women everywhere who are calling upon the name of the Lord. I pray my Father even in the midst of anger we will not be compelled to sin. I pray in the name of Jesus that the historical lies that have divided us will be exposed by the Holy Spirit and through the word, the wisdom of God healing would come and flow. I take authority in the name of Jesus over every spirit of division and hindrance would try to undo the move of the Holy Spirit that is purposed to the church of Jesus Christ in the United States of America and across the world because what affects these nations affects nations everywhere and nations and worlds are watching. In the name of Jesus I take authority over the spirit of division. We pull down the racial lie in the name of Jesus. We speak healing, wholeness, and soundness to the people of God everywhere. Lord like You did in John 17:17 – Sanctify them by Your truth. Your word is truth. I am not praying for everybody now, but I am praying for the church. I am praying for the people of God.

Father I am praying for sons and daughters of God and I decree in the name of Jesus You, Lord will give us beauty for ashes and the garment of praise for the spirit of heaviness. I pray for every African- American mother who is afraid to let her children to gout. I pray for every African American man and woman everywhere who are festering with injustice and anger. Father, I pray in the name of Jesus that You, Lord minister healing. I pray for well meaning, good-hearted, and well-intentioned white brothers and sisters and any other ethnicity who really want to be a part of healing and helping, I pray in the name of Jesus that You, Lord would bring people with answers together supernaturally. I ask for this and believe I receive it. I thank you for it in the name of Jesus, Amen.

I have just hit something in the Spirit that is key to healing of ethnic divide. God has purposed a move of His Spirit that is going to bring a great deal of healing, wholeness, and wellness. That is one of the reasons why they do not want the church to get together now. It is not natural. God is up to something, and the enemy is trying to sow discords and divisions, but in the name of Jesus we take authority over the spirits of discords and division.

Chapter 7

Intimacy with god and Fellow Man

God made man in His image, likeness, similitude, and resemblance to have fellowship with him forever. Genesis 1:26- 28…and 2:14…God's intention was for closeness, familiarity, nearness, inseparability with the man He made. The relationship was emotional warmth or closeness. It is a quality that suggests informal warmth, friendship, or closeness. Something that is very personal or private. The first man (male and female) was intimate with God. God would visit with them in the cool of the evening which also was exemplified in their intimate relationship. When man sinned, that intimacy was eroded. Sin separated him from God, and he was to live in that state of separation from God forever. So, God had to find a temporary solution in the case of Adam and Eve before He could find a permanent way of redeeming mankind and restore him to everlasting abundant life. The way God redeems is by offering sacrifice. When Adam and Eve sinned and discovered for first time that they were necked they put leaves together and covered themselves. In order for God to start dealing with man again He had to offer some sacrifice. So, God sacrificed some animals for the sin committed and clothed man with the skins to cover their nakedness. God was speaking and Satan understood what God was saying. God was promising man that He was going to redeem him eventually. At that moment God was functioning in the dimension of horse. The horse is in the family of lamb. Jesus was in the lamb that was slain before the foundation of the world. Hebrews 1:14. The angels minister to us when the Godhead is deciding how they are going to express themselves to His creation because there was the problem of separation by sin. Creation worship God when they see His glory but they have never been close to Him to interact with Him at that level since the fall of man. They do not know Him at that level of glory. They just see His brightness and bow down. The problem the Godhead face is how God was going to express Himself to His creation because they had seen Him. They could not approach Him because if they saw Him in their fallen state they would be consumed. God dwells in an unapproachable life. Therefore, there is no way you can approach God in that unapproachable life. Now God had to find a solution and man was that solution. He created man in His image so man could show forth and reflect God such that creation could look at man and see how God operates because man could carry the dimension of God. Just imagine if a cherubim could be so powerful that it came down and take son in its hand and could distinguish the son from the palm of His hand with that kind of power. Then how much powerful is mankind if he could carry dimensions of God. Man can carry dimensions of God than the cherubim.

The cherubim reflects the power of God. Man

can reflect the dimensions of God more than a cherubim. Really living in this world should not be a problem to us. We should be walking in the dimensions of God such that we become unmorally in our community, society, and country because the normal problems that every human being faces we should be overcoming those issues. We should be walking in the dimensions of God such that we are far beyond what the world can present us with. The problem that mankind has to do with intimacy with God, being close to God. Enoch demonstrated closeness with God. The scripture says that Enock walked with God before God took him up to His presence. But before God took him, he had this testimony that he pleased God. Without faith it is impossible to please God. Those who come to Him must believe that He is a rewarder of those who seek Him diligently. So, Enoch grasped that concept of intimacy with God and fellow man.

Throughout the years the problem has been intimacy with God so we can be intimate with our fellow man. Enoch understood that if he continued in intimacy with God, God was going to give him the desires of his heart. God Himself will give you the desires of your heart. Desires of our hearts is the reward God gives us. It is our inheritance from the Father. The riches and wealth are evidence that we have some power, but the reward is the inheritance. It is vanity to have the evidence of the power without the power itself. God told Abraham, "I am your exceeding great reward". This is the nature of closeness of God with mankind. Now there is an intimacy issue because people desire to walk in the dimensions of God's power, but they substitute that by trying to prosper their way. The material prosperity is just a small token of what we should have when we are walking in the dimensions of God that make this world bow down to God. Lack, sickness, death, strife and hatred should be able to bow down to God. Everything in this world should be able to bow down when we walk in the dimensions of intimacy with God. So, you get your inheritance when you step out into that dimension of power of God. Everything in the world has to bow down to the nature of God in you and me.

Galatians 4:6-7 states that – *"⁶And because you are sons, God has sent forth the Spirit of His Son into your hearts, crying out "Abba, Father!" ⁷Therefore you are no longer a slave but a son, and if a son, then an heir of God through Christ. ⁸But then, indeed, when you did not know God, you served those which by nature are not gods. ⁹But now after you have known God, or rather are known by God, how is it that you turn again to the weak and beggarly elements, to which you desire again to be in bondage? ¹⁰You observe days and months and seasons and years. ¹¹I am afraid for you, lest I have labored for you in vain.*

Fears for the Church

¹²Brethren, I urge you to become like me, for I became like you. You have not injured me at all. ¹³You know that because of physical infirmity I preached the gospel to you at the first. ¹⁴And my trial which was in my flesh you did not despise or reject, but you received me as an [e]angel of God, even as Christ Jesus. ¹⁵*[f] What then was the blessing you enjoyed? For I bear you witness that, if possible, you would have plucked out your own eyes and given them to me.* ¹⁶*Have I therefore become your enemy because I tell you the truth?* ¹⁷*They zealously court you, but for no good; yes, they want to exclude you, that you may be zealous for them.* ¹⁸*But it is good to be zealous in a good thing always, and not only when I am present with you.* ¹⁹*My little children, for whom I labor in birth again until Christ is formed in you,* ²⁰*I would like to be present with you now and to change my tone; for I have doubts about you.*

Two Covenants

²¹*Tell me, you who desire to be under the law, do you not hear the law?* ²²*For it is written that Abraham had two sons: the one by a bondwoman, the other by a freewoman.* ²³*But he who was of the bondwoman was born according to the flesh, and he of the freewoman through promise,* ²⁴*which things are symbolic. For these are [g]the two covenants: the one from Mount Sinai which gives birth to bondage, which is Hagar—* ²⁵*for this Hagar is Mount Sinai in Arabia, and corresponds to Jerusalem which now is, and is in bondage with her children—* ²⁶*but the Jerusalem above is free, which is the mother of us all.* ²⁷*For it is written:*

"Rejoice, O barren, You who do not bear! Break forth and shout, You who are not in labor! For the desolate has many more children Than she who has a husband. ²⁸*Now we, brethren, as Isaac was, are children of promise.* ²⁹*But, as he who was born according to the flesh then persecuted him who was born according to the Spirit, even so it is now.* ³⁰*Nevertheless what does the Scripture say? "Cast out the bondwoman and her son, for the son of the bondwoman*

shall not be heir with the son of the freewoman." [31]So then, brethren, we are not children of the bondwoman but of the free."

All creation is your inheritance. The dimensions of God are your inheritance. Until we realize who we are and what we have and how to operate in that dimension we shall continue walking as slaves in God's sufficiency. Until we realize what we have and are possible and walk in those possibilities by the revelation of Christ we shall be operating beneath our privileges. When we are able to grasp the revelation of Christ in this dimension then and only then can we begin to enjoy life in its full meaningfulness. If we do not grasp the revelation of Christ in here, we shall not walk in that revelation. We must get the revelation of Christ and download it in our life. We download the revelation of God in and by prayer of faith and walk as incorruptible seed not as corruptible seed which is the word of God that abides forever. The revelation of Christ in you will download things from God and begin to walk in those dimensions He is. The place of downloading is the place of intimacy with God in prayer and study of the word. So, the dimensions that you can walk in are available to you, however there is a price to pay. You must pay the price. Jesus paid the price for your salvation and made the way so you may have intimacy with God. That intimacy is going to cost you time. You must sacrifice your time at the altar of consecration where you spend time with God. The time you could have gone to spend watching movies, but you decide to spend with God. The time you could have spent on meals, but you choose to spend it in prayer and fasting. The time you could have done a lot of other things you decide to spend it in the presence of God. When you want to have something precious you sacrifice by the word of God which lives and abides forever. That incorruptible seed, new spirit in you has been given by Jesus Christ to download things from God and begin to walk in the dimensions of God. The place of downloading is the place of intimacy in prayer. The dimension of power of God is available, but there is a price to pay. You must pay the price of walking in the power dimensions of God. Jesus Christ paid the price of removing the obstacle that hindered operating and walking in the power of dimensions of God. That intimacy is going to cost you time. If you are going to maintain intimacy with God you will have to sacrifice your time at the altar of consecration. When you desire intimacy with God you will spend time with God in study of the word, prayer, sacrifice food, and fast. When you find something precious you sacrifice everything to get it. To follow Christ, we must first deny ourselves of everything and take His cross upon us. The fear or reverence of the Lord produces honor, riches, and abundant life and requires humility.

Luke 18:1 states that – *"Then He spoke a parable to them, that men always ought to pray and not lose heart"*

When you are always in prayer and study of the word God is downloading His image, likeness, resemblance and similitude into you. He is downloading His character, nature and authority in your life and you are looking more like Him perpetually. Evil spirits will be repelled by the presence of God with and in you. The solution to all issues of life is dwelling in the secret place of the Almighty.

Psalm 91:1 states that – *"He who dwells in the secret place of the Most High Shall abide under the shadow of the Almighty"*

When you are in prayer you take the position of an eagle. Your ascent or rise upward to the presence of God.

According to Isaiah 40:31 – *"But those who wait on the LORD Shall renew their strength, they shall mount up with wings like eagles, They shall run and not be weary, they shall walk and not faint"* and Revelation 12:14 – *"But the woman was given two wings of a great eagle, that she might fly into the wilderness to her place, where she is nourished for a time and times and half a time, from the presence of the serpent"*

The eagle comes down and picks up the serpent and takes him out of its natural habitat into the air and destroys its place of intimacy or environment. When Christians ascent into the presence of God, sorcerers, witches, wizards, diviners and demons as well ascent to Satan's altar. That satanic altar comes against Christians who ascend to God. The agents of axis of evil become monitoring spirits and set ambushes against the praying Christians. But the good news is that demons cannot find you when you are in God's presence.

Revelation 12:1 state that - *"Now a great sign appeared in heaven: a woman clothed with the sun, with the moon under her feet, and on her head a garland of twelve stars".*

John the Revelator was a man of intimacy with God. We must be saved by force and power to exhibit the dimensions of God. In the above quoted scripture woman represents the body of Christ, the bride of Christ. She is clothed with the sun. The sun represents the glory of God. The moon represents the powers of darkness under her feet. When the church comes to a place where they are clothed with the glory of God all the powers of darkness are subjected under her feet.

She begins to make the agents of axis of evil bow down to her feet. These agents of axis of evil reflect hell. They impose the kingdom of darkness upon the earth. All the evil we see in the earth is a manifestation of the kingdom of darkness. The argument we see between husband and wife who God joined has to do with a witch or wizard somewhere who wants them to break. The wizards and witches throw spells at them to become like them and one of them or both stop praying in the spirit. Now they get into the house and start fighting over a toothpick. Their attention is now redirected from God to other things for lack of intimacy with God.

Chapter 8

Testing Positive For Faith

In the book of Daniel chapter 10 the bibles states that when Daniel set himself to seek God the angel was dispatched and when the angel gets to Daniel, he says "The prince of Persia withheld me. I am delighted you are reading because the word of God is coming to you in an immensely powerful and significant way. You are going to test positive for faith not for coronavirus. It is time to stand up for Jesus while everyone else is running away from pandemics. When you understand God's word and a pandemic comes you will know how to deal with it to defeat it. If it does not come near you will know how to keep it at bay. I believe with all my heart and spirit that God is speaking to His people this hour. He wants us to come to a deeper level of understanding of the times and of knowledge about what it is that you and I are to be doing as new creations in Christ Jesus in the earth and as covenant believers in the earth. In this chapter, we are writing on the end of the age, who, and what is coming upon the earth. With the Coronavirus pandemic that has swept across the globe a lot of people are in a state of uncertainty and fear. They are not sure of what is happening and what is coming upon the earth. They are wondering whether this is the end of the world, end of the age, is Jesus coming or is somebody else is coming? What is coming? People of all walks of life have now begun asking questions, what is happening? Those who have been sensitive in the spirit can sense something is changing in the environment around us. The world now feels vastly different than it did in previous years. I believe there is spiritual shifts in the atmosphere and the bible tells us about them. The prophets of old foretold of coming these days. End days and time has been talked about asking the question, what does that look like and when is it supposed to happen? I am going to write about something the Spirit of God has revealed concerning you and your household. God is preparing a people who will not only be ready to meet Him, but people ready to do in the earth what they are called, anointed, and assigned to do before that day He comes again.

The end of the age, what, and who is coming upon the earth.

There are some questions believers have been asking themselves and this is not the time to be uncertain about the things in the word of God. This is the time that you should know what you are to speak about, believe, and expect.

Matthew 24:3 states that – *"Now as He sat on the Mount of Olives, the disciples came to Him privately, saying, "Tell us, when will these things be? And what will be the sign of Your coming, and of the end of the age?"*

Jesus' disciples are asking for the signs of the times and the end of the age. We are talking about the end of the age and the world. In this verse 3 – Jesus has just been asked three different questions *When will these things be? what will be the sign of Your coming? and of the end of the age?"* The response that He gives is in the following verses 4 – 14 are answers to those three questions. Some of the things Jesus said have been fulfilled and the others are yet to be fulfilled. Jesus had just predicted in the verses that precede this one. He had prophesied and told the disciples about the destruction of the temple in Jerusalem, the temple that they walked by every day, they were familiar with, where the secretariat and priesthood functioned in Judaism. There was a temple there that was standing up to Jesus' death, burial, resurrection, and His ascension. This temple was the center of worship in Jerusalem and Jesus had spoken about the temple being destroyed. So when they asked the question "When will these things be" it was about the destruction of the temple. Then they asked what would the signs of His coming be and what will be the signal of the end of the age?

That gives you some insight into the coming of the Lord or Jesus' coming and the end of a specific age that they are talking about are connected. In Verse 4 Jesus, now goes to speak about those things. These things or signals are not the end of the world, but the end of the age. In verse 9, now Jesus is speaking to those disciples that are standing before Him and each one of them was persecuted and died in an incredibly significant and marcher-like way except John the Revelator. According to verse 14, when these signals happen there will be some level of preaching the gospel and instruction that will have begun to be preached.

This gospel of the kingdom is the gospel of the rule, realm, and royalty of God. The gospel of good news or the principles that govern the operations of the anointing in the earth so that God's People can operate in that anointing and dominion God promised them. Regardless of what is coming in the earth they will be operating in dominion. That is the hour we are in now.

I believe this coronavirus pandemic is one of those perilous pestilences Jesus spoke about in the scriptures that requires a season of sobriety and a higher level of standing for men and women of God to preach, teach and instruct God's people how to overcome, stay above only and operate in the anointing that ceases every yoke and bondage of devils and demons to be dispelled and ejected. That is the gospel that must be preached all over the world as a witness to all nations and then the end will come.

Jesus connects the end of the age that He is being asked about to the preaching or the fullness of the preaching the gospel of the kingdom. That gives you and I some connection and understanding about the end of the age He is addressing. He says at the end that age this gospel of the kingdom is going to be preached and that is going to be a signal of the end of the age and His coming.

Now we are going to have to deal with the coming of the Lord because He coming, but we got to understand the coming of the Lord and what that actually means as the scripture refers to it. According to the scripture, Jesus is coming first to catch away His church and in that coming He will not set His foot on planet earth. That will begin a seven-year period and at the end of that seven-year period Jesus is coming and this time He is coming with His saints and that is the time He will put His foot on the planet Earth. That is the time according to the scripture called millennial reign will appear. When we talk about the coming of the Lord we must distinguish between when He is coming for the saints (catching away of the church) and when He comes with His saints. He is going to get them in what is called the Rapture. The word rapture is never used in the scripture. You will not find it anywhere in the scripture. The fact of the matter is that Jesus is coming to catch away His church, that is to seize and catch them up. After the saints are with Him for seven years of earthly time passage and at the end of that period, He will come again to set up His millennial reign. So the first time He comes to get the saints and the second time He comes with the saints after seven years. It is important we understand these things because we are right now in this period of time where these things are going to begin to happen and come upon the earth.

Luke 21:7-24 - The Signs of the Times and the End of the Age

⁷So they asked Him, saying, "Teacher, but when will these things be? And what sign will there be when these things are about to take place?"

⁸And He said: "Take heed that you are not deceived. For many will come in My name, saying, 'I am He,' and, 'The time has drawn near.' Therefore, do not go after them. ⁹But when you hear of wars and commotions, do not be terrified; for these things must come to pass first, but the end will not come immediately."

¹⁰Then He said to them, "Nation will rise against nation, and kingdom against kingdom. ¹¹And there will be great earthquakes in various places, and famines and pestilences; and there will be fearful sights and great signs from heaven. ¹²But before all these things, they will lay their hands on you and persecute you, delivering you up to the synagogues and prisons. You will be brought before kings and rulers for My name's sake. ¹³But it will turn out for you as an occasion for testimony. ¹⁴Therefore settle it in your hearts not to meditate beforehand on what you will answer; ¹⁵for I will give you a mouth and wisdom which all your adversaries will not be able to contradict or resist. ¹⁶You will be betrayed even by parents and brothers, relatives and friends; and they will put some of you to death. ¹⁷And you will be hated by all for My name's sake. ¹⁸But not a hair of your head shall be lost. ¹⁹By your patience possess your souls.

²⁰"But when you see Jerusalem surrounded by armies, then know that its desolation is near. ²¹Then let those who are in Judea flee to the mountains, let those who are in the midst of her depart, and let not those who are in the country enter her. ²²For these are the days of vengeance, that all things which are written may be fulfilled. ²³But woe to those who are pregnant and to those who are nursing babies in those days! For there will be great distress in the land and wrath upon this people. ²⁴And they will fall by the edge of the sword and be led away captive into all nations. And Jerusalem will be trampled by Gentiles until the times of the Gentiles are fulfilled.

In Matthew's account he emphasizes that this gospel of the kingdom will be preached in all the world (cosmos – decorations, arrangements, and props). In other words, it is going to be preached in all the systems of the world. That is especially important because the political system, economic system, entertainment system, health system, education system, religious system, etc (the kingdoms of the world) are going to be penetrated with the message of the gospel the kingdom of God. The people who are going into those systems and areas demonstrate the gospel of the kingdom and the superiority of life in Christ Jesus and living by the word of God by faith in the son of God. It is going to be demonstrated in the earth that there are people of God who are living by His word and the things that are coming on the rest of the world are not affecting them because they are standing on God's Word. This is what Jesus prayed in John 17 before He went to the cross. He said, "I pray that You do not take them out of the world but that You may keep them above the evil that is in the world". In John 17:17 Jesus said "Sanctify[a] them by Your truth". And then He said, "Your word is truth". So, when these things that are coming upon the earth the gospel of the Kingdom, those men and women who are living by the word, standing by the word, and living by the word of God are going to be separated and distinguished by that word, the truth they are living by. Disease will come but will not come near their dwelling. Economic downturn will come but they will prosper and increase. People everywhere will be afraid, but those who know their God will be strong and do exploits.

This is the word of God and He said again and again darkness will come upon the earth, but you shall arise and shine for your light has come and the glory of the Lord is risen upon you. This is what is happening right now in the earth. The question now is if it is gonna happen which side are you going to be on?

Luke 21 is Luke's account of the same event, an inquiry that the disciples made in Matthew 24 that Matthew recorded. Luke records it a little differently and says things that are important. Luke includes information that Matthew does not that makes it truly clear that Jesus is responding to more than one question. Therefore, it is important for us to notice and understand the importance of Jesus' response. Like Matthew records, Luke records that Jesus was speaking to the disciples who were present with Him at the moment. *Luke 21:24 – "And they will fall by the edge of the sword and be led away captive into all nations. And Jerusalem will be trampled by Gentiles until the times of the Gentiles are fulfilled."* This is a powerful statement because it begins to give us insight to what Jesus is talking about in Matthew 24 when He says at the end of the age that **"This gospel of the kingdom shall be preached to all nations of the earth then the end shall come."** This is the end of a specific age. The Greek word "I ON" means a cycle, system or modality, a way of life is going to come to an end. Luke gives us an insight as to what way of life is coming to end and what season that is. People who are not a seed of Abraham according to the flesh are gentiles. What does is it mean "until the time of gentiles are fulfilled?" The time you and I have known is this age. The only age you have ever lived in is this one that is about to come to an end. What you and I are sensing is shifting of the end of the age. This age has been going on since Jesus since Jesus came to the earth. When the times of the gentiles are getting ready to be fulfilled, there will be signs in the Sun, Stars, and Moon. (In Genesis Sun, Moon, and Stars) were for times, seasons and signals of the end of the age or signs of the times of the gentiles being fulfilled.

Chapter 9

-----••◆••❧•᠙🙚🙚᠙•❧••◆••-----

The Coming of the Son of Man

²⁵"And there will be signs in the sun, in the moon, and in the stars; and on the earth distress of nations, with perplexity, the sea and the waves roaring; ²⁶men's hearts failing them from fear and the expectation of those things which are coming on the earth, for the powers of the heavens will be shaken. ²⁷Then they will see the Son of Man coming in a cloud with power and great glory. ²⁸Now when these things begin to happen, look up and lift up your heads, because your redemption draws near."

As this time of the gentiles begins to be fulfilled, as that age begins to come to an end the nations will begin to be in distress. There will be distress of nations so perplexing among the nations and there will be no answer. What is happening is that the powers of the heavens, the principalities and powers, the rulers of darkness of this world that operate in that heavens, in that unseen realm. There are some ruling principalities over nations and they are going to begin shifting because revelation knowledge is coming on the earth. The revelation knowledge is shaking them. The wisdom of God is beginning to be released in the earth. Jesus said, in these last days the knowledge of the glory of God will begin to cover the earth like the waters cover the sea. What is happening is that there is a deluge of the revelation knowledge and instruction. God's people are beginning to inquire of Him and seek Him and the power of the heavens are beginning to be agitated. When the powers of heaven begin to be agitated it causes things on earth to be shaken. One of the reasons why coronavirus pandemic has hit the earth is that devils are agitated. Revelation knowledge is coming because the furniture in heaven is being shifted or rearranged and the King is about to appear. God is just displaying His power because He has it. It is the signal of the end of the age. Jesus said He is coming and it is settled that He is coming. I do not know about you, but I shall be going up with Him with first load.

There are two loads going and I have chosen to be in the first one. There is one time when Jesus shall come with power and glory and there is another time He is coming with tens of thousands of His saints. The first time He comes without the saints and the second time He comes with the saints because He will have taken the up. They shall have been with Him and they shall be with Him. That is why Paul says in that first load" And we shall forever be with the Lord". Once He catches you away wherever He goes you go.

Jesus gives us some significant insight now in Matthew 24 and in Luke 21 about what age is ending and about the times of the gentiles being fulfilled.

In Daniel 2 we begin to understand the end of the age from divine biblical and historical perspective. From her we are going to see what age is coming to an end. You and I are the children of the most high God, we have been all our life, what is called the church age or the gentile age. The bible says that Jesus of Nazareth came so that those of us who were not of the seed of Abraham according to the flesh might be partakers of the covenant that God made with Abraham.

(Galatians 3:13, 26 13 Christ has redeemed us from the curse of the law, having become a curse for us (for it is written, "Cursed is everyone who hangs on a tree"), 26 For you are all sons of God through faith in Christ Jesus.)

When you understand what is coming to an end you understand what the coming of the Lord is all about. It is more than theater; it is more than God flexing His muscle. It is God putting the spotlight on the truth that has been articulated throughout the ages concerning His son. Paul is speaking to the church at Galatia which is primarily made of non-Jewish people who have come to Christ through the preaching of the gospel. This is one of the reasons why the New Testament is written mostly by Paul, the apostle. Most of his epistles and letters are written to non-Jewish people.

The reason why Christ came is so that the blessing and the covenant that God put on Abraham and the Jewish nation might come on the rest of the world through the believing in Christ Jesus. In Galatians 3:26 Paul is speaking to non- Jewish people who have come to Christ through the preaching of the gospel. When you come to Christ there is therefore no Jew or Greek, but there is now a new creation. In relation to the covenant and Christ there is no disparity. Christ Jesus came so that those of us who were not born of the natural seed of Abraham according to the flesh might through Christ Jesus who is the seed of Abraham come into the covenant and not be missed or alienated. Jesus the Christ calls us to the covenant so we are not without God and hope in the world. Therefore, Jesus came so that those of us who were non-Jews come into the same covenant that God made with Abraham and have access by one Spirit of the Father.

Therefore, Jesus' time and the preaching of the gospel is so that the non- Jews people can come into this covenant that God made with Abraham. God has allotted a time a and season for that preaching to be done so that the nations of the world who may come into relationship with Him can do so then that time is going to come to an end. That is what the coming of Lord is about. It is a signal that the season of the gentiles coming into the covenant is coming to an end. According to the scripture there is another age that is going to begin that will include a number of things including the man of sin, the beast, the great evangelization of the Jewish nation and people as   Paul says in *Romans 11:26* – *"And so all Israel will be saved, as it is written: "The Deliverer will come out of Zion, And He will turn away ungodliness from Jacob."*

Right now, this time you don't see a great number Jewish people coming to Jesus, but they are going to come in great numbers. Now is the age when the harvest of the gentiles are coming in. That is why Luke 21:24 is saying "….. And Jerusalem will be trampled by Gentiles until the times of the Gentiles are fulfilled". This season of the non-Jewish people coming to Yahweh through Jesus will happen.

Romans 11:1 - I say then, has God cast away His people? Certainly not! For I also am an Israelite, of the seed of Abraham, of the tribe of Benjamin. ²God has not cast away His people whom He foreknew. Or do you not know what the Scripture says of Elijah, how he pleads with God against Israel, saying, ³"LORD, they have killed Your prophets and torn down Your altars, and I alone am left, and they seek my life"? ⁴But what does the divine response say to him? "I have reserved for Myself seven thousand men who have not bowed the knee to Baal." ⁵Even so then, at this present time there is a remnant according to the election of grace. ⁶And if by grace, then it is no longer of works; otherwise, grace is no longer grace. [a]But if it is of works, it is no longer grace; otherwise, work is no longer work.

⁷What then? Israel has not obtained what it seeks; but the elect have obtained it, and the rest were blinded. ⁸Just as it is written:

"God has given them a spirit of stupor, Eyes that they should not see and ears that they should not hear, to this very day."

Paul is a Jewish man but he has received grace to preach to non-Jews primarily. Paul is reasoning from the past to the present that God in His response to Elijah was foreshadowing the future saying even though you think all my people have deserted me, they have not. Now get the plan of God. He is saying through the rejection of the Jewish nation of Jesus, God has made space for the gospel to be preached to the non-Jew that is, the nations of the earth. The plan of God is that by the goodness of God to the nations, all Israel will be provoked to come to Him. Paul was aware of the fact that his ministry was primarily during this season where the gentiles are being called to God. Those who have come to Christ have come through the Jewish nation for the Jewish nation was given the covenant of promise as was first committed the gospel and you and I who are non-Jews have heard the gospel because some Jew accepted of the gentiles the gospel and preached to us. Now this is what we are getting near. We are getting near the time where the fullness of the gentiles comes in. Those of us who have been preaching the gospel going to church thinking things are going to stay this way for ever have not understood we have been custodians of season of the time that is to come to an end. Jesus gave us the indications that world signify the end of the age. You and I are looking at the end of the gentile age. *Daniel 2:27-44 – "Daniel answered in the presence of the king, and said, "The secret which the king has demanded, the wise men, the astrologers, the magicians, and the soothsayers cannot declare to the king. [28] But there is a God in heaven who reveals secrets, and He has made known to King Nebuchadnezzar what will be in the latter days. Your dream, and the visions of your head upon your bed, were these: [29] As for you, O king, thoughts came to your mind while on your bed, about what would come to pass after this; and He who reveals secrets has made known to you what will be. [30] But as for me, this secret has not been revealed to me because I have more wisdom than anyone living, but for our sakes who make known the interpretation to the king, and that you may [a] know the thoughts of your heart.*

[31] "You, O king, were watching; and behold, a great image! This great image, whose splendor was excellent, stood

before you; and its form was awesome. ³²This image's head was of fine gold, its chest and arms of silver, its belly and [b]thighs of bronze, ³³its legs of iron, its feet partly of iron and partly of [c]clay. ³⁴You watched while a stone was cut out without hands, which struck the image on its feet of iron and clay, and broke them in pieces. ³⁵Then the iron, the clay, the bronze, the silver, and the gold were crushed together, and became like chaff from the summer threshing floors; the wind carried them away so that no trace of them was found. And the stone that struck the image became a great mountain and filled the whole earth.

³⁶"This is the dream. Now we will tell the interpretation of it before the king. ³⁷You, O king, are a king of kings. For the God of heaven has given you a kingdom, power, strength, and glory; ³⁸and wherever the children of men dwell, or the beasts of the field and the birds of the heaven, He has given them into your hand, and has made you ruler over them all—you are this head of gold. ³⁹But after you shall arise another kingdom inferior to yours; then another, a third kingdom of bronze, which shall rule over all the earth. ⁴⁰And the fourth kingdom shall be as strong as iron, inasmuch as iron breaks in pieces and shatters everything; and like iron that crushes, that kingdom will break in pieces and crush all the others. ⁴¹Whereas you saw the feet and toes, partly of potter's clay and partly of iron, the kingdom shall be divided; yet the strength of the iron shall be in it, just as you saw the iron mixed with ceramic clay. ⁴²And as the toes of the feet were partly of iron and partly of clay, so the kingdom shall be partly strong and partly fragile. ⁴³As you saw iron mixed with ceramic clay, they will mingle with the seed of men; but they will not adhere to one another, just as iron does not mix with clay.

⁴⁴ And in the days of these kings the God of heaven will set up a kingdom which shall never be destroyed; and the kingdom shall not be left to other people; it shall break in pieces and consume all these kingdoms, and it shall stand forever."

It is in Daniel's vision that one of the reasons people read the book of Revelation and don't fully understand Daniel's interpretation of the vision. You cannot really fully come to comprehend the type and the shadow of revelation and disclosure in the book of Revelation. You really cannot begin to understand the beast and the false prophets of the time if you don't fully understand some things about Daniel's interpretation of Nebuchadnezzar's vision in Daniel chapter 2. Nebuchadnezzar who is the king of Babylon has had a dream. He at this time is the most powerful ruler on earth and his nation is the most powerful nation on earth and at this time the bible says he goes to bed in inquiring about the kings that are to come and as he goes to sleep he has a dream and a vision. He sees this image with head of gold and various parts of the body are of different materials. The vision so disturbed him and called all the astrologers, soothsayers, the wise men in his kingdom of Babylon and all the provinces and tells them that they must not only interpret his dream but they must tell him what the dream was. He gets frustrated because no one can tell and interpret the dream and the vision and says he was going to kill all of them. Mishaal, Hananiah, and Azariah whom we know as Daniel Meshack, Shadrack and Abednego were the three Jewish boys who had been brought to the king and Daniel had already distinguished himself. He is one of the wise men in the king Nebuchadnezzar's kingdom who is about to be put to death. And when they came to kill Daniel because he is one of the Wisemen and no one had been able to tell the dream and its interpretation, Daniel tells them hold on. Let me inquire of God, let me seek God and God will give me, not only the interpretation of the dream, but the dream itself.

Daniel tells the king "What you have seen is the disclosure of what will be in the later days." Daniel answers an incredibly significant question. God gives a pagan king who is not serving Him a dream and interpretation of things that are gonna happen in the last days. The question is why does God give such a dream to Nebuchadnezzar who is a political leader, not a prophet, not even a covenant man. He is a politician, a king, and a ruler, but at this moment he is the top world leader of his time. He is currently the custodian of God's prophetic people. The nation of Israel, God's people are under Babylonian captivity. In our time God's prophetic people has been the church in the nation of the United States of America for a long time. God gave Daniel an interpretation of the dream for the sake of His people Israel. God is saying and doing some things right now. He is giving insight, revelation, and interpretation to His servants in the nations of the earth for His people, the church. That is why the answers are not coming to political leaders. They are coming to God's servants. When you watch the news the politicians don't know what to tell you. But there are God's servants who are hearing directly from the Spirit of God concerning what time it is now. If you want the good news now you will have to watch some else other than the news media. They do not have it. There is a higher level of understanding the things to come.

Daniel by the Spirit of God has revelation and told the king what he dreamed. Daniel is speaking to a man who is not a prophet, not in covenant with God, but Daniel is telling him he is the king of kings and God has given him the kingdom, power and strength. God has the ability to put men in places of authority even though they don't know him, serve him, have no covenant with Him for His reasons to cooperate with His plans for the end of the age.

Because you, Nebuchadnezzar are the ruler of the most powerful nation on the earth of your time, whatever you do, wherever there are people, wherever there are birds of the air, and whatever you know will influence them. That kind of power and ability is given to nations by God for reasons and seasons of God. United States for years has enjoyed it, but she did not understand why! She sees the blessing, favor, and prosperity of God not because she was United States. Blessings and favor were in the United States for a reason and season of time. She was the number one custodian of the preaching and propagation of the gospel to the nations. That is why she was blessed. She was not blessed because she had intelligent presidents, congress nor because she was the holiest nation on earth. She was stewarding the gospel and spreading it across the world and any nation that does that will have the blessing of the Lord. At this time Nebuchadnezzar was stewarding God's prophetic people. He was allowing them to function in the midst of his kingdom and God had given him blessing for it.

Daniel gives Nebuchadnezzar the interpretation of the dream that the images he had seen, head of gold, legs and thighs of bronze, and chest and arms of silver that these are nations, empires and he was the head of gold. Daniel tells him that after him there was going to be a second kingdom, inferior to his and a third of bronze that will rule over all the earth. A fourth kingdom shall be as strong as iron that will break in pieces and crash all others. The kingdom shall be divided into just as he saw the feet and toes partly a part of clay a partly a part of iron and yet the strength of iron shall be in it. The kingdom shall be partly strong and partly fragile.

Daniel has just interpreted Nebuchadnezzar's dream that Nebuchadnezzar had the dream of the nations and the empires of the earth that would rule and exist until the end of the gentile age.

Here below is a list of the empires of the world that have biblical impact.

Empires Of The World That Are Referenced As Having Biblical Impact Following Nebuchadnezzar's Dream

1. Egypt 3,100 to 30 BC

   a. Babylon Below 1792 to 1595 BC

   b. Assyria - 1244 to 612 BC

   c. Persia – 550 to 224 BC Achaemenid and Sossaman

2. Greece - 461 to 323 BC {Athenian and Macedonia}

3. Rome {Roman/European} - 264BC to 476 AD – *[From global policy forum - Dates are interpretive and meant to be suggestive. Author A Paul]*

These empires of the world which have had biblical impact are biblically referenced in the scripture and had impact relative to Daniels's vision.

The first is the Egyptian empire that had already been before Nebuchadnezzar's dream. The second is the empire of Babylon which is followed by Assyria and the Persia. These makeup what is called the Persian empire. The fifth is Greece and the sixth one is Rome.

God says to Nebuchadnezzar the empire he is in

is gold which is Persian that really covers Babylon, Assyria and Persia. That is the empire of gold. The next kingdom to him which is inferior is Assyria and Persia. The fourth kingdom is Rome which was to be as strong as Iron and was to crash in pieces all others. Rome was the most powerful empire on earth, and it covered all the known world and shuttered every other empire that preceded it. I believe by the spirit of God that speaks of two natural and spiritual. Rome not only became a political empire but also a religious empire when Constantine who was the emperor was converted to Christianity and calls the Roman empire the official religion to become Christianity. The kingdom is split both naturally and spiritually. It also became both a political and a religious empire and Christianity became the official religion of the Roman empire to the point that even if you were not really converted people began saying they were Christians because they wanted to get along with the dictates of the then emperor, Constantine.

In Daniel 24:43 - As you saw iron mixed with ceramic clay, they will mingle with the seed of men; but they will not adhere to one another, just as iron does not mix with clay.

What happens there is that when that empire becomes split it begins to give birth to a hybrid. As the Roman empire splits between the two regions, East and West it also begins to take a political and religious formalism which gives birth to the only Roman empire of the catholic church. What happens now during that time is that the catholic church and the only Roman empire begins to be the religion.

The word catholic means "universal". It is not a denomination, it means worldwide. The pope begins to determine who the kings are of the nations of the earth primarily in Europe which is the inhabited world. So now the kings derive their power from Rome, from the pope, from Vatican. This is the mixture of Clay and Iron being referred to in Daniel's vision. What begins to happen in Rome is birthing Europe as power through people's authority. The Vatican and the holy Roman Empire, the catholic church, the spirit of the Roman Empire lives in it.

It is a conquering kingdom and gives birth to European authority on the earth,
{Spain, Rome, and other European states} begin to be the most powerful nations on earth through this mixture of politics and Religion. Now the European nations begin to intermarry. Kings and the nations begin to intermarry so that the English king is related to the French king and the French king is related to the Australian king, and the Australian king is related to the Russian king. They are all intermarrying and receiving their authority from Rome. So, the spirit of the Roman Empire is still ruling Europe. It is a spirit, and it is the key element that ruled during the time of gentile age. Therefore, Europe became one of the prosperous regions on earth because they became the custodian of the gospel and they became that religion that disseminates the gospel throughout the whole earth. It shifts from Europe to

England and shifts from Great Britain to United States of America. The United States of America becomes the custodian of the gospel and the nation that disseminates the gospel throughout the world. That is one of the reasons it is prospering.

Daniel 24:44 – "And in the days of these kings the God of heaven will set up a kingdom which shall never be destroyed, and the kingdom shall not be left to other people. It shall break in pieces and consume all these kingdoms, and it shall stand forever."

What Daniel says is that at the end of this time of mixture, as the age of these gentile kings begins to end the God of heaven is going to set up His kingdom that will never be destroyed. When the God of heaven begins to establish His kingdom these other kingdoms and these kingdoms of the Gentiles are going to be shuttered. They are not going to be left for other people, but they will be broken into pieces. You and I are watching the shuttering of the kingdoms the gentiles. They are coming to pieces.

Chapter 10

What Shall We Do Now?

PRAYER

Father, we bless You such a time as this and we thank You. We honor and magnify You because there is no other name greater than Yours. We appreciate Your presence knowing that Your presence makes the difference. Thank You for Your people. Thank You for the integrity of Your word. Grant us this time that we worship as we celebrate and gather around Your word, that we are not only better, but we are transformed. We know the power that transforms is the living word of God. Thank you for all that shall be written and read in this book.

We declare victory and liberty is ours. We declare the curse of the finished work of Jesus, no weapon that is formed against us can prosper. Every tongue that raises against us is already condemned. This is a part of our inheritance as Your sons in the earth, and we declare our righteousness comes from You. We count it done. Thank you for it. In Jesus name, Amen.

Studies show, unless you understand your role in society, you can never make any meaningful contribution. According to the Greeks there are three types of people on earth, the idiots, the tribesmen, and the citizens. Studies show only 10% in communities are citizens. The remaining 90% are either tribesmen or idiots.

When the Greeks used the word *"IDIOT"*, they did not use it as a curse word. Idiots are people who just don't care!

If they write exams, they will cheat. If they are in government, they will steal. An idiot does not care at all, if he eats bananas, he throws the peels anywhere instead of putting them in a trash bin.

According to the Greeks, some societies have more idiots than tribesmen and citizens. The next set of people are tribesmen, these are people that look at everything from the point of view of their TRIBE. These are people that believe in you only if you are part of their tribe. It can be terrible to have a tribesman as a leader, he will alienate the rest. When the Greeks talk about tribes, it's not just about ethnicity, RELIGION also is considered as a tribe.

A great percentage in the society are tribesmen, because they view everything from the point of view of their tribes. They trust only their tribesmen. The last group are citizens. These are people that like to do things the right way. They will respect traffic light rules even if no one is watching them. They drive within speed limits.

They respect the laws, won't cheat in exams. In government they won't steal. They are compassionate and give to others to promote their wellbeing. Citizens often promote projects that benefit everyone. The

Greeks called this group the citizens. Some countries have more citizens than tribesmen and idiots. Others have so many idiots. A Tribesman can become a citizen through orientation. And an Idiot can become a citizen by training and constant enforcement of the law. But things fall apart if you elect an idiot or tribesman to lead you if he has not been reformed. Where do you belong? Are you an idiot, a tribesman or a citizen? Reflect about your LIFE. Reflect about your country and world in general before you answer. Food for thought.

Right now, so many things are taking place in this three-dimensional material world and moving at a breakneck speed and yet there is a consistency and constancy that you and I as believers have in the word of God. The bible declares the word of God is alive and powerful. Jesus said "before one jot (comma or period) would be changed from the word heaven and earth would pass away. So, we have an anchor in the word of God. The thing about the word of God is that as we move into the word of God we are constantly coming into new dimensions of the truth. Not that the truth changes, the truth does not change, but our ability to process and understand the layers that we come to in the understanding the truth of the word of God should be constantly growing and going into deeper depths and higher heights in God's word. I believe the Holy Spirit has arranged and ordained this moment in time for you and me to make quantum leaps in the understanding and application of the word of God. I am excited about our future on what God is saying to us by His word and we want to make sure we get the word of God in book format. You and I are a prophetic community of which is that remnant within a nominal church that is constantly hearing from God and understanding the responsibility to declare and speak God's word and make transformative change. The coronavirus pandemic and the uprising that is happening right now in the United States for social and societal change have come as a surprise and yet the spirit of the Lord is always ahead of anything that happens and given instruction on what needs to be done.

There is power in the name of Jesus and I know by the Spirit of grace something good is going to happen to you. God has planned it, the Holy Spirit is orchestrating it, and I am writing to declare to you that if you do not give in, you are on your way up and out of whatever has attempted to keep you down. There is something about the name of Jesus. During all that is going on in the earth I declare loud and clear, I am unabashedly unapologetically a Christian. I believe in the power of the name of Jesus. I believe in the power of the blood of Jesus. I believe that Jesus is the equalizer. He is the one who causes things to come into proper alignment in in lives as we dare to believe Him.

Matthew 5:12-16; 38-45 {12Rejoice and be exceedingly glad, for great is your reward in heaven, for so they persecuted the prophets who were before you. 13"You are the salt of the earth; but if the salt loses its flavor, how shall it be seasoned? It is then good for nothing but to be thrown out and trampled underfoot by men.

14 "You are the light of the world. A city that is set on a hill cannot be hidden. 15 Nor do they light a lamp and put it under a basket, but on a lampstand, and it gives light to all who are in the house. 16 Let your light so shine before men, that they may see your good works and glorify your Father in heaven.

38 "You have heard that it was said, 'An eye for an eye and a tooth for a tooth.' 39 But I tell you not to resist an evil person. But whoever slaps you on your right cheek, turn the other to him also. 40 If anyone wants to sue you and take away your tunic, let him have your cloak also. 41 And whoever compels you to go one mile, go with him two. 42 Give to him who asks you, and from him who wants to borrow from you do not turn away. 43 "You have heard that it was said, 'You shall love your neighbor and hate your enemy.' 44 [n] But I say to you, love your enemies, bless those who curse you, do good to those who hate you, and pray for those who spitefully use you and persecute you, 45 that you may be sons of your Father in heaven; for He makes His sun rise on the evil and on the good, and sends rain on the just and on the unjust.}

These are the words of Jesus and His teachings have been erroneously misunderstood that has led the church as a whole and the Christian individual voice specifically to be passive in the light of conflict when Jesus is not teaching a passive response at all. Jesus is teaching something else. He does not want you to be hit on both sides of your face. The word "Son" in Hebrew does not refer to gender but it means one with the nature, character, and authority of another. So, Jesus is saying, I am instructing you to do these things so that you may have, demonstrate, manifest, and display the character, the nature, and authority of your Father who is in heaven.

Now that there has been clearly identifiable, and broadcast image of injustice in the nation. What God is doing and speaking through His Spirit is applicable to the church everywhere, there is now something we must do about the uprising, protest in the street some of it has become riotous, but that is not the essence of the protest. Most of the protest is peaceful, it is civil unrest for the purpose of transformative change which is by in large an American right and privilege granted to us by the Constitution and bill of rights. Therefore, protest that which is unjust is a proper and accurate response when you see things in the nation that are out of line not only with the word of God but out of line with tenets that the nation has set forth for itself. We have now seen in all industries change that are denoting something is changing and shifting. We cannot forget that all of this has occurred during a global pandemic. We are seeing now in this nation re reality we are in throws of a cultural revolution.

There is a revolution that is going on. Dr. martin Luther King said "a social movement that only moves people is merely a revolt, but a movement that changes both people and institutions is a revolution." When he wrote that he was reflecting on a civil rights sermon in 1963 "Thy kingdom come, Thy will be done". When social change and protest in the streets regarding the injustice and the freedom call for the things of the civil rights movement that he was the prophetic voice in not just a civil rights leader. Dr. King was a prophet and one of the things we must retrospect realize is that if we are going to see any kind of forward movement in the injustice is that the wind behind the civil right movement of the 1960s was a prophetic wind. One of the reasons it advanced so is because there was a Spirit of God behind it not just civil, it was spiritual. It was not led by a civil rights leader, but a prophetic voice who had such a powerful gift of utterance and understanding of times that his prophetic articulation went out into civil functionality. That is what we need again in the United States of America and in that regard the church of Jesus Christ must be a part of it.

Today we are seeing in every sector, system, and individual's world there is a responsibility being demanded and a set of new responses must be made. We are in a moment of sweeping societal and social change and the church of the Lord Jesus Christ will not be exempted. The church of Jesus Christ will not be exempted from this demand for change. The change is being called for in every sector of society right now from broadcast journalism to policing, social structures, economic powers and to political structure. Every system is being shaken. In every system there is a demand for change. The church of Jesus Christ must change in her addressing the issues of the day. In many ways the church is partially responsible for the transgenerational perpetuation of the lie of racism in the United States of America because she has chosen to parrot and propagate the ideology and the nomenclature of the politics of colonialism and imperialism rather that to proclaim the wisdom, truth, and the perspective of the kingdom of God. There is one race God created, the human.

Leviticus 17:11- For the life of the flesh is in the blood, and I have given it to you upon the altar to make atonement for your souls; for it is the blood that makes atonement for the soul.'

Acts 17:23-26 - [23]For as I was passing through and considering the objects of your worship, I even found an altar with this inscription: Therefore, the One whom you worship without knowing, Him I proclaim to you: [24]God, who made the world and everything in it, since He is Lord of heaven and earth, does not dwell in temples made with hands. [25]Nor is He worshiped with men's hands, as though He needed anything, since He gives to all life, breath, and all things. [26]And He has made from one blood every nation of men to dwell on all the face of the earth and has determined their preappointed times and the boundaries of their dwellings.

There is one race, human and within that one race there is a diverse ethnic, mosaic that God has created for His own purpose and pleasure. Whether you realize it or not God is pleased by my color and by the fact that I am not like everything and everyone else. God is pleased by your color too and if we understand that the issue is not the color of your skin, but it is the condition of our spirit, and soul that is at dilemma. Therefore, the preaching of the gospel is necessary, but not the preaching of traditional western European cultural religion that we have adopted as Christianity but preaching of the actual truth of the word of God. We must now stop the articulation of division of racism and start saying what God says. You say it and everyone else so says it here that there is only one race, human.

Anybody who says anything else is not preaching the truth of the word of God. It is in some ways right that a generation has rejected us in this area because we have not been telling the truth. Somebody now must lift their voice and say, "what shall we do now"? We are amid a revolution and as I look into the word of God it has occurred to me that Jesus was a revolutionary. It is pathetic that His church has become passive and mundane when its founder was a revolutionary. The prophetic community must look into the word of God and do it with a revolutionary attitude.

Matthew 5 is Jesus' sermon on the mount which we call sermon in biblical school and theology class. It is Jesus' initial introduction to His ministry and initial introduction of His purpose and perspective to the people that He is preaching to. The sermon on the mount is Jesus's opening soliloquy of ministry and what He is about to start. What is interesting about the sermon in the mount is the beatitudes. The essence of the beatitudes is that Jesus is announcing that whatever condition you find yourself in, you can be blessed because He is there.

Matthew 5:21-22, 27,31-34 & 38-39 - 21"You have heard that it was said to those of old, 'You shall not murder, and whoever murders will be in danger of the judgment.' 22But I say to you that whoever is angry with his brother without a cause shall be in danger of the judgment. And whoever says to his brother,

'Raca!' shall be in danger of the council. But whoever says, 'You fool!' shall be in danger of [h] *hell fire.* [27] *"You have heard that it was said to those of old, 'You shall not commit adultery.'* [31] *"Furthermore it has been said, 'Whoever divorces his wife, let him give her a certificate of divorce.'* [32] *But I say to you that whoever divorces his wife for any reason except* [i] *sexual immorality causes her to commit adultery; and whoever marries a woman who is divorced commits adultery.* [33] *"Again you have heard that it was said to those of old, 'You shall not swear falsely, but shall perform your oaths to the Lord.'* [34] *But I say to you, do not swear at all: neither by heaven, for it is God's throne;* [38] *"You have heard that it was said, 'An eye for an eye and a tooth for a tooth.* [39] *But I tell you not to resist an evil person.*

Jesus starts a set of statements I call "You have heard, but I say" statements. He has said several times, "you have heard, but I say".

Jesus the revolutionary says what you have heard is not actually accurate. What you have been taught in your religious traditions is not actually a fulfillment of the mind and purpose of God. Jesus the revolutionary comes and says, you have been hearing this all your life. You have been attending church, doing daily reading, and daily meditations, but I have come to say to you, I did not come to wreck it, I came to fulfill it, I did not come to wreck it, I came to cause you to understand what it really means.

The Spirit of God right now is calling on the church worldwide to leave its traditions and live out of the truth of the scripture in this area. If the church fails to make the change and transformation in the near future the church will be irrelevant because this is a pivotal moment. If the issues that are swirling around preachers in the current day are not a part of the computative process and spiritual preparation you are missing the beat. Something supernatural is happening and as for me I say that the body politics of racism is currently on the operation table and before she dies let us Xray the body and discover the history and the origin of this spirit of racism so that before she dies, we can extract it all unless she mutates and some other devil arise that is hard to put to death. Now is the time to deal with it. We have got to recognize that we have heard so much but now is the time to look at what the scripture says about these things. Jesus begins this series of statements where He says, "you have heard, but I say, you have heard, but I say, and you have heard, but I say." What is he doing, He is making and marking a revolutionary moment. He is drawing a line in the sand between up to now and from now on. Jesus is converting erroneous historical religious understanding for current social response and action. You have heard this, but this is what I am telling you to do. If that is true "what shall we do now?" It is from this series of statements that I have inquired of the Lord and received instructions not only for me but for everyone who has ears to hear.

Matthew 5:38 says, [38]*"You have heard that it was said, 'An eye for an eye and a tooth for a tooth."*

Jesus speaks to His followers, to people who are going to be following Him and who are going to be living in the world, but not to be a part of the world. That does not mean you are not to interact with it, or not to speak to it. It does not mean you are not going to try to change it. What it means is that you cannot change it with the weapon that they are using. You are going to have to employ another set of weapons that you only have.

2 Corinthians 10:4-6 says, - "[a]For the weapons of our warfare are not [a]carnal but mighty in God for pulling down strongholds, 5casting down arguments and every high thing that exalts itself against the knowledge of God (against the knowledge that the scriptures have given to you), bringing every thought into captivity to the obedience of Christ, 6and being ready to punish all disobedience when your obedience is fulfilled."

Casting down imaginations literally means erroneous arguments and conclusions of religious men and demons. I am in favor of protest, picket, and resist. But when Jesus says "do not resist an evil person it sounds very non-confrontational. We need to eradicate this lie. Christianity is not a non-confrontational ideology, but it is a powerful mechanism as Dr. Martin L King said, "non-violent resistance in love is more powerful than swords and spears." It emanates and manifests the reality of a superior spiritual individual because it takes more than to walk in love than it does to throw a brick. Probably you are saying author, I am fed up and I have had enough. I am a Christian and I need to do something and yes, we all do. Notice what Jesus says in Vs 38 and 39 - *38"You have heard that it was said, 'An eye for an eye and a tooth for a tooth. 39But I tell you not to resist an evil person".* It sounds non-confrontational, but Jesus is not teaching do not confront evil. He himself confronted evil. There was a time He went in the temple and overturned the tables of the money changers. This is not a passive cat. It is not an individual who is just willing to gallop with the gang and let anything fly. No! This is someone who understands what it means to be confrontational. Notice what Jesus is teaching and this what the prophetic community must understand.

What Jesus says, "DO NOT RESIST" what he is saying is that do not allow negative action. By negative I do not mean bad. Resisting is not a bad action. What Jesus is speaking to is this, Resistance action is initiated by the doer of it. When I resist you, I have given power to your action. I am responding to your action. It is negative activity. Jesus says do not allow anyone to bring you into negative activity.

When some offense comes against you, do not allow the offender to have the power because all you are doing is responding to the offender. There is a higher agenda that the offense. There is a purpose and it has to be corrected. There is a soul that has to be transformed and there is a mind that has to be renewed. Jesus is teaching us that when you resist your action of resistance is a continuation of the offender's action. Jesus is saying when someone comes for your eye or your tooth convert the aggression and the injustice of your opponent into positive action of resolve and social action. He is saying do not let anybody back you into just responding. In other words, tell your opponent I am not here just to respond into your injustice. I am here to call you to a higher level not only of thinking but a higher level of living. That is what Jesus' cam and died for that is what his church must model. (2:17:39. video)

You can exercise your civil right to protest resist with the social action of the day, but couple your resistance with prayer and standing on the word and speaking the word of truth and word of life because it is going to take more to bring the transformation that just walking around and resisting. I know this is not popular and is why I am writing this truth down because the scriptures tells us you know the truth and that truth shall set you free. We must stand for what the scriptures say and teach even when I need to be converted in order to agree with it. Jesus is telling us to convert the aggression and injustice of the oppressor into resolute positive social action. When Jesus says turn the other cheek, He is saying respond from the side of the part of you that has not been touched. You hit me in an area, you say you know what I have another whole part of me the you cannot even get to. I have got another whole dimension of me that you cannot even see. I have a whole power on the inside of me not just the responsive. I have a higher agenda and call than getting back at you. Respond from the part of you that cannot be touched. That does not mean just be spiritual but it means respond with your gift. This is important because it doesn't matter what anybody does to you, they cannot take your talent, ability and the gradual endowment that God has given you. The very best thing you can do is respond with your gift and prosper whether people want or not. Rise whether people like it or not, write the book, write the song do the play, and do what God has put on the inside of you. Because the reality of the Christian life is that nobody can keep you down when your father has made a way for you. Maybe you are a youth and you are wondering what must I do. Well, what is your gift, calling, talent, and the gradual endowment that God has given? It is the thing that you have that you did not pay for and no man gave you and no one can take away from you. Jesus is saying don't let anybody make you, their victim. You make sure that you respond out of the gift of God that is on the inside of you.

One of the things that Dr. Martin Luther King Jr. said is that, The old order ends no matter what bastille or prescience remain when the enslaved within themselves bury the psychology of servitude." That means an agenda or ideology ends, whatever people are trying to do to you and against you ends when you within yourself bury the psychology of being a victim and understand nobody can stop you, keep you down, the gift, the call and the anointing in you from rising to the top. Greater is He that is in you than he that is in the world. Jesus is teaching something that er who believe this gospel must absolutely let out.

Matthew 5:40- The question here is that what shall we do now. You cannot get bitter, angry, and not let your anger lead you to something positive, coherent or congruent. The Bible in Ephesians 4:26 says "Be angry and do not sin, do not let the sun go down on your wrath." There is nothing wrong with being angry just don't let your anger move you to negative action, but let anger cause the greater one on the inside to rise up, the gift, the calling, and anointing in you rise. Now is the time to do what God has called you to do and do it with favor. There is an open door for what is in you to come out. The fact of the matter is that the spirit of God liberty is behind you and there is nothing that can stop your rise. If God is for you who can be against you. The question is not whether somebody will be against you, if God is for you whoever is against you will have to move out of the way. If the spirit of God is backing what you are doing then whoever is trying to resist it is no longer just resisting you they are resisting God. Now is the time for what is in you to come out strong and write your song, book and do your thing. Jesus is saying reverse the energy of the one who is trying to take from you. Become the giver in the wake of people trying to take from you. Jesus is not saying that you let somebody chain and drug you to enslave you. He is saying even if somebody wants to use the law to come against you (sue you) don't allow that negative energy to consume you. Jesus says you become the giver. Give to the world what is yours to give. What is your contribution, moves, motivates and what is yours that only you can give. The fact of the matter is if you are paying attention to more of what is going on in the world there is something inside of that is warming and the spirit of God is saying that is from Him. Jesus says do not only give but give more than they thought you were capable of producing. Manifest more than they thought you had you had within you. May I tell you there is some stuff within you that is about to come out that people are going to be surprised when it manifests. If you would listen to the spirit of God on the inside of you and spend time in prayer with God you are going to find purpose in these moments. You are going to find something that only you can do that nobody can take from you.

In whatever discipline you are in now is the time to inquire of the Lord what shall I do with this gift that is within me. If you seek Him He will empower you to give more than you thought you could and to do more than you thought was humanly possible with what is inside of you.

Now is the time to move and act in positive action and the wind of the spirit of God is going to cause you to sail into waters you thought you could never move into.

Luke 17:1-5, You must understand not only who you are but where you are and what the spirit of God is going to do in you and through you if you allow Him in this revolutionary moment. Jesus Himself is opening a dialogue with the disciples and says "It is impossible that offense should come and He the same Jesus who said with God nothing shall be impossible. It is because now you not only dealing with men because He knows what is in the hearts of men only those who have not been born again, but let us be real. There is some stuff in the mind and conscience of people that have been born again that needs to be transformed.

The spirit of God is doing that in the church you and I will not be exempted from being demanded of every sector of the society we are going to have to change. The change is not going to be an eradication of the principles of the word of God. It is a father understanding and fulfillment of the truth of the Word of God.

Now don't be surprised when you start thinking in ways you wouldn't have thought ten years ago. Jesus is saying to every follower of His that you are going to be offended. He just promised you somebody is going to wound you, hurt you and mistreat you unjustly. It is impossible that offense should come. But woe to Him through whom offense comes. Every time you see the word woe in the scripture it is an announcement of the curse coming upon an individual. What does it mean to be cursed. We are not talking about witchcraft and incarnation. The word curse means to have the disregard of. An individual who is under the curse or dealing with a curse is someone who has the disregard meaning not having the cooperation of the Spirit of God you must understand that it is impossible that you live without being mistreated. It is impossible that you will live and not encounter injustice. It is impossible that you will live and not bias. But Jesus is saying whoever comes against you has my disregard. Whoever tries to fight you has my disregard. God will not fight for him who fights against you. God will not back him who opposes you who are doing His will and walking by His word. God is whoever comes against you comes against Him and they have His disregard. This is what

God meant when He said to Abraham "Anybody who blesses you I am with them and if they curse you, they have my disregard." When you understand that then you don't have to retaliate to every injustice when God is your Father and the Spirit of God is upon you. You don't have to take every matter into you own hands. I know this that when you come against me you have His disregard. I watch Him handle it.

This is a part of the confidence the child of God has. It is important for you and I who believe the word of God to now declare the word of God in this area. I am not talking about your car or money, but I am talking about the protection of your son or mother. I am talking about how you deal with injustice in society around you. If this gospel is not good for that then it is good for nothing.

If we are not going to believe it in this area then let us do something else. I am not waiting for justice after life here on earth. When you do the word of God you will see the hand of God move in your situation. Now I have been stopped by police and falsely accused for moving violations several times but you know what I have a covenant with God.

V3. This is perhaps one of the most counter-intuitive seemingly contacting instructions that the word of God can give and the reason it is that way is because it goes against all the religion we have been taught where they say don't pay attention to yourself and do not do anything for yourself: when it comes to being offended, treated unjustly defrauded and taken advantage of notice what Jesus says. The moment you get offended the most important person in the word of God is you. He says take heed to yourself. This is the moment where God gives you and I as Christians the right to pay attention to ourselves. What are the instructions or what is He saying? Pay attention to yourself with the understanding, knowledge and wisdom that the offense that has come against you is a trap. The word used here for offense is the Greek word scandalon where we get the English word scandal which means a trigger or a trap. What Jesus is teaching whenever an offense, injustice, someone attempts to take advantage of you politically or socially and in any other way, He said pay attention to yourself because it is a trap to stop your forward momentum and suppress your gift calling and you're anointing. It is a trap to divert your attention away from what you should be doing to retaliating. It is a trap and do not take it or step on it. I am not the only one writing on the basis of the Word of God, but also on the basis of years of experience of following Jesus and I can tell you in no uncertain terms that your greatest times of offense, mistreatment when you want to retaliate and when you want to get into your own flesh and do it come just before your greatest promotion elevation, open door opportunity. They come to blind you from what is about to lift you up. They come to keep you from that transformative change that the Spirit of God has been working on you for years and I am pleading with you do not miss this revolutionary moment because God is about to raise you, He is about to lift you, open the door for you and He is about to remove your offenders out of your way and enemies of your path. He is going to make a way for you if you will trust Him and His word and lean not on your own understanding and go the way of the world. Jesus was responding to this when He said do not take the trap. Confront it. But do not confront it negatively, deal with it in a positive action. Then Jesus if your brother repents if he changes not giving lip service But bringing forth fruits worth repentance then you forgive and start walking because nobody can stop what God is about to do for you. The offense, the anger, the emotion, and the desire to retaliate in your flesh is a trap to keep you from your moment of elevation. This is the place when the disciples heard Jesus say this when He told them, when you get offended this is how you need to respond, this is how you deal with it, this is how you need to take it. This is the place where the twelve guys who were following Him said "Increase our faith." I pray for you to get faith increased of course. I understand that faith does not just come because the word of God does not just come because we ask for it. It comes because the because the Word of God comes to us. We must get the word of God and get it in our mouth. I am having to do this because I know as sure as I am writing this book that you are about to be elevated.

I know doors are about to open for you. I know that an adversary is about to be put down for the very last time and you will see them no more. I know that your child will be protected, healed, and come back. I know that they are going to get their education. I know the world that they grow up in will be better than this one. I know something will supernatural is about to change and my God is on the throne. I know Jesus is at work and His spirit is working and the church has an opportunity to be relevant if it will allow itself to be changed, transformed and honest. I refuse to allow everybody else to have a say in what happens next, and the church has no voice. We must stop talking about race and work the word of God. We must stop discussing lies because neither one of us will win and no one will get closest to the truth. We must be righteously indignant We must get tired of the hypocrisy of people who want to do the word in every other place but when it comes to this, they keep perpetuating the lie that their ancestors perpetuated. This is now our normalcy. I don't know about, but I have been waiting for my moment this is it and I have divine backing. 1 lie has short legs, and it will soon run itself to death. We must now preach and teach this next generation that God made one race, human. Change happens when the mind is transformed. The mind is renewed and transformed by trying to change it, but when we make the proper presentation. When we say what God's, word says. – Romans 12:1-3 May the Spirit of God lead you to the words that you need to hear. Know will be revealed to you and God put it in your mouth so that this revolutionary moment you can demonstrate the nature character and the authority of your Father. You and I have authority, Jesus said He gave you authority to tread upon serpents and scorpions so that nothing by any means shall harm you.

Prayer: Father in the name of Jesus I pray right now for the church of the Lord Jesus. I pray for your servants around the globe. I pray for Apostles, Prophets, Teachers, Evangelists and Pastors that the truth of the word will be what they begin to proclaim in this area. Where the world by its fallen intellect and wisdom has propagated the lie of race. Father let the church not lift its voice and say there is one race and God loves the diversity that God created. You said that you created all things for your pleasure. You made all the colors to please you. There is something that you love about diversity. Father, in the name of Jesus, I pray now for the church everywhere that as transformation, cultural and societal change happens around us in every realm, endeavor, sector, and system. I am asking you in the name of Jesus to bring change and transformation to the churches and pulpits around the globe. I believe I receive it and I stand on your word.

You said no good thing will you withhold if we walk upright. You said if we ask anything according to your will you will give us. I know it is your will that this divide may be healed and therefore I am asking for it and I believe I receive it. Now I pray for men and women of color in the church who are dealing with offense hurts, wounds, and hatred anger in the name of Jesus. Lord I pray that they see the trap exposed and what it is. I ask in the name of Jesus to increase their faith and lead them to the word they need to the promises the need, cause your spirit to speak in theirs so they hear what you want them to hear and know what you want them to know. In the name of Jesus, I pray for every ethnicity that is deserving to be a part if the healing and the solution that must happen in the church, Father in the name of Jesus bring us together in unity, brethren dwelling together in unity. You said you command the blessing where brethren dwell together in unity. Father, I set myself in agreement with your word in the name of Jesus. Father I pray for the gift, calling in them, the anointing the gracious endowment of God Ask for it did they get it by education may come to fruition. May they know beyond the shadow of a doubt that no weapon formed against them can prosper. Anyone who comes against that unique thing you put in them will find themselves opposing you may they opponents have your disregard. Father I pray that when they step out by faith and do according to their gratuitous endowment will bring healing not only to situations, but they are going to bring prosperity to them and their families. Cause them to arise to a higher level. Father I know prosperity is important because when they have what they need they can do what You have purposed for them to do. Father, I pray for the youth who are wondering what they should do now with their gifts and talents. I pray for those who have failed them, those in church who have left them, and they are irrelevant. I pray oh God that You rescue these gifts, anointings, callings and work with them for Your purpose. I pray in the name of Jesus, that whatever is hindering and standing against my brethren from using their gifts to do their assignment, I ask in the name of Jesus that according to Your word that You cause every valley to be exalted and hill brought low that the way may be prepared for what they are purposed to do in You to manifest in this hour and season. Father, I know I am praying according to Your will and I know I have it in the name of Jesus, Amen.

Chapter 11

Potential for Prejudice in the Christian Heart

There is a potential for prejudice in the Christian heart because that reality is something that believers and Christians at large have not examined or entertained the possibility of prejudice. We think that when we are believers in Christ, washed in the blood of the lamb, church goers, and preachers so immediately and without fail certainly there is no prejudice in our hearts, minds, and we are born again. The fact of the matter is that the scriptures do not bear out that premise. What we need to see is that the Spirit of God has included in the cannon of scripture so that those of us who must deal with these issues can do so in truth and bring about dialogue and discussion.

God is up to good things concerning the new creation believer and we should expect those things to manifest in our lives as we do God's word. There is a lot of information in Acts chapter 10 that is germane to the subject that we are going to address and we cannot take for granted that every reader is so familiar with the study that they can follow it along and yet I also don't want to prevail too much upon your reading although I do want to make sure that I communicate as best as I can what is required for us to understand the dynamic of this biblical narrative and how it relates to the Spirit of the Lord who wants you and I to know, receive, process, and understand. Please understand that there are some things the Spirit of the Lord is directing us to write and deal with that are somewhat uncomfortable. These things must be dealt with in this time and moment because the Spirit of God is urging and leading us into a moment that I believe the church of the Lord Jesus Christ in the earth must recognize, embrace, and participate in them. One of the things impressed upon me is international conversation on ethnicity and what the world calls race. Again the "Race" is a fictitious misnomer yet to dismantle a lie you must at times utter them.

The subject of "race" as it is discussed in the 20th and 21st century mindset is a historical lie. The bible does not speak about race in relation to the distinction of ethnicity or color between people. In Acts chapter 17 the scripture says Paul under the inspiration of the Holy Spirit says God has made from one blood all nations of men to dwell upon the earth. So, there is one race, human race. Within that race there are distinct ethnicities od ethnic groups. The historical lie of race that has been perpetuated and propagated in the 20th and 21st centuries primarily in the west is a creation of men who on one end say *"We hold all these truths to be self-evident that all men are created equal that they are endowed by the creator with certain alienable rights among these are life, liberty, and pursuit of happiness"* and the same time the subject other men and women to slavery. To do that with good Christian conscience if you are going to say that all men are created equal if you are going to say that they endowed by their creator with certain inalienable rights that means the rights to liberty is not something men give to you. It is something God gives you. That they are endowed by their creator with inalienable rights and among these are life, liberty, and pursuit of happiness are rights God gives. So, you cannot pen that in your decoration of independence and then be a slave owner, holder, codify and cannonade slavery in your constitution and in your nation without first of all subjecting the person you are enslaving to something less that human. You have first to make them less than you to enslave them and still say all men are created equal.

Therefore, there is the creation of this other race in the mind and mentality of men, but it is not in the mind of God. As I have said before the word "Race" is not a divine concept, biblical concept and it is not a Christian concept and yet the church of the Lord Jesus Christ has taken the nomenclature and perpetuated it not making the distinction the bible makes. Therefore, they have not brought healing to this dialogue and matter. They have further accentuated and perpetuated the vision. I believe the Spirit of God wants to bring healing and reconciliation to it. This cannot be done unless we first gather around the truth which the word of God. Jesus declared that the Word is Truth. Therefore, in that sense God says in *Amos 3:7-8 that "Surely the Lord GOD does nothing, Unless He reveals His secret to His servants the prophets. A lion has roared! Who will not fear? The Lord GOD has spoken! Who can but prophesy?"*

There is something that is happening right now in the spirit realm. I believe God is speaking and those of us who have the responsibility of ministering the gospel of the kingdom must prophesy in line with what the Spirit of God is doing and saying in the nations of the earth.

Acts 10:1-45 and - There was a certain man in Caesarea called Cornelius, a centurion of what was called the Italian Regiment, ²a devout man and one who feared God with all his household, who gave [b]alms generously to the people, and prayed to God always. ³About [c]the ninth hour of the day he saw clearly in a vision an angel of God coming in and saying to him, "Cornelius!" ⁴And when he observed him, he was afraid, and said, "What is it, lord?" So, he said to him, "Your prayers and your alms have come up for a memorial before God. ⁵Now send men to Joppa and send for Simon whose surname is Peter. ⁶He is lodging with Simon, a tanner, whose house is by the sea. He[d] will tell you what you must do." ⁷And when the angel who spoke to him had departed, Cornelius called two of his household servants and a devout soldier from among those who waited on him continually. ⁸So when he had explained all these things to them, he sent them to Joppa. ⁹The next day, as they went on their journey and drew near the city, Peter went up on the housetop to pray, about[e]the sixth hour. ¹⁰Then he became very hungry and wanted to eat; but while they made ready, he fell into a trance ¹¹and saw heaven opened and an object like a great sheet bound at the four corners, descending to him, and let down to the earth. ¹²In it were all kinds of four-footed animals of the earth, wild beasts, creeping things, and birds of the air. ¹³And a voice came to him, "Rise, Peter; kill and eat."

¹⁴But Peter said, "Not so, Lord! For I have never eaten anything common or unclean."¹⁵And a voice spoke to him again the second time, "What God has [f]cleansed you must not call common." [16] This was done three times. And the object was taken up into heaven again.

[17] Now while Peter wondered within himself what this vision which he had seen meant, behold, the men who had been sent from Cornelius had made inquiry for Simon's house, and stood before the gate. [18] And they called and asked whether Simon, whose surname was Peter, was lodging there.

[19] While Peter thought about the vision, the Spirit said to him, "Behold, three men are seeking you. [20] Arise therefore, go down and go with them, doubting nothing; for I have sent them."

[21] Then Peter went down to the men [h]who had been sent to him from Cornelius, and said, "Yes, I am he whom you seek. For what reason have you come?"

[22] And they said, "Cornelius the centurion, a just man, one who fears God and has a good reputation among all the nation of the Jews, was divinely instructed by a holy angel to summon you to his house, and to hear words from you." [23] Then he invited them in and lodged them.

On the next day Peter went away with them, and some brethren from Joppa accompanied him. [24] And the following day they entered Caesarea. Now Cornelius was waiting for them and had called together his relatives and close friends. [25] As Peter was coming in, Cornelius met him and fell down at his feet and worshiped him. [26] But Peter lifted him up, saying, "Stand up; I myself am also a man." [27] And as he talked with him, he went in and found many who had come together. [28] Then he said to them, "You know how unlawful it is for a Jewish man to keep company with or go to one of another nation. But God has shown me that I should not call any man common or unclean. [29] Therefore I came without objection as soon as I was sent for. I ask, then, for what reason have you sent for me?" ³⁰ So Cornelius said, [i] "Four days ago I was fasting until this hour; and at the ninth hour I prayed in my house, and behold, a man stood before me in bright clothing, ³¹ and said, 'Cornelius, your prayer has been heard, and your [j] alms are remembered in the sight of God. ³²Send therefore to Joppa and call Simon here, whose surname is Peter. He is lodging in the house of Simon, a tanner, by the sea. [k]When he comes, he will speak to you.' ³³So I sent to you immediately, and you have done well to come. Now therefore, we are all present before God, to hear all the things commanded you by God." ³⁴Then Peter opened his mouth and said: "In truth I perceive that God shows no partiality. ³⁵But in every nation, whoever fears Him and works righteousness is accepted by Him. ³⁶The word which God sent to the children of Israel, preaching peace through Jesus Christ— He is Lord of all— ³⁷that word you know, which was proclaimed throughout all Judea, and began from Galilee after the baptism which John preached: ³⁸how God anointed Jesus of Nazareth with the Holy Spirit and with power, who went about doing good and healing all who were oppressed by the devil, for God was with Him. ³⁹And we are witnesses of all things which He did both in the land of the Jews and in Jerusalem, whom [m]they killed by hanging on a tree. ⁴⁰Him God raised up on the third day, and showed Him openly, ⁴¹not to all the people, but to witnesses chosen before by God, even to us who ate and drank with Him after He arose from the dead. ⁴²And He commanded us to preach to the people, and to testify that it is He who was ordained by God to be Judge of the living and the dead. ⁴³ To Him all the prophets witness that, through His name, whoever believes in Him will receive remission of sins." ⁴⁴ While Peter was still speaking these words, the Holy Spirit fell upon all those who heard the word. *45 And those of the circumcision who believed were astonished, as many as came with Peter, because the gift of the Holy Spirit had been poured out on the Gentiles also.*

Acts 11:1-18 - Now the apostles and brethren who were in Judea heard that the Gentiles had also received the word of God. 2 And when Peter came up to Jerusalem, those of the circumcision contended with him, 3 saying, "You went into uncircumcised men and ate with them!" 4 But Peter explained it to them in order from the beginning, saying: 5 "I was in the city of Joppa praying; and in a trance I saw a vision, an object descending like a great sheet, let down from heaven by four corners; and it came to me. 6 When I observed it intently and considered, I saw four-footed animals of the earth, wild beasts, creeping things, and birds of the air. 7 And I heard a voice saying to me, 'Rise, Peter; kill and eat.' 8 But I said, 'Not so, Lord! For nothing common or unclean has at any time entered my mouth.' 9 But the voice answered me again from heaven, 'What God has cleansed you must not call common.' 10 Now this was done three times, and all were drawn up again into heaven. 11 At that very moment, three men stood before the house where I was, having been sent to me from Caesarea. 12 Then the Spirit told me to go with them, doubting nothing. Moreover, these six brethren accompanied me, and we entered the man's house. 13 And he told us how he had seen an angel standing in his house, who said to him, 'Send men to Joppa, and call for Simon whose surname is Peter, 14 who will tell you words by which you and all your household will be saved.' 15 And as I began to speak, the Holy Spirit fell upon them, as upon us at the beginning. 16 Then I remembered the word of the Lord, how He said, 'John indeed baptized with water, but you shall be baptized with the Holy Spirit.' 17 If therefore God gave them the same gift as He gave us when we believed on the Lord Jesus Christ, who was I that I could withstand God?" [18]When they heard these things, they became silent; and they glorified God, saying, "Then God has also granted to the Gentiles repentance to life."

Please notice that Cornelius was an Italian, not a Jew. He is a God-fearing man, but he is Jewish in his ethnicity. He was a giver and prayed to God always. The angel tells Cornelius to send a man to Joppa. There is a man there by the name Simon Peter (one of the apostles of Jesus Christ) was a man who walked with Jesus, who heard what Jesus said, who saw the miracles Jesus did. Cornelius is praying in one place and peter in another place. Cornelius, who is non-Jew, gets direction from the angel to send men to Joppa to find peter and he will tell you what to do. While the men are coming peter goes up on house top to prayed. Peter does not know what God told Cornelius and has idea that men are coming. While in prayer peter gets a spiritual vision. Peter a is good Jewish man. The thing he is seeing being let down are all things that the law of Moses says they are unclean to engage with or to eat. Peter being a good Jewish man raised in a kosher lifestyle. He has never touched or eaten anything that in his traditional religious understanding has determined. It is not anything he is going to deal or engage with. So, when he sees this vision and hears a voice telling him rise peter slay and eat, his response is out of religious traditional training and understanding and says no I have never eaten anything unclean or participated in that kind of a thing. He is basically saying my tradition and religion has taught me this way and I do not deal with that. God is saying to him what has happened in the earth through the finished work of Jesus has changed what your understanding of your responsibility should be regarding that which before you have not engaged with. Peter is under the direction of the Holy Spirit. He has just met these men who have come to him from Cornelius' house. He does not know them or why they have come. All he knows is that he had this vision that he doesn't fully understand that is challenging his traditional religious upbringing and the Spirit of God says to him there are three men coming to you go with them and don't doubt anything I sent them. God is going to take him on a journey and if peter was going to follow Him. He was going to lead him into something that was going to challenge his mind, heart, and will without actually knowing what was going on. I submit to you that now the Spirit of the Lord is doing that very thing with the church of our Lord Jesus Christ and people globally. He is leading us into areas that are unfamiliar and untraditional that go beyond our traditional that go beyond our traditional religious and ethnic upbringing to bring healing and a solution. When Peter gets t Cornelius' house he knows as a Jew he is not supposed to enter a gentile's house. This is an ethnic issue. It is a traditional and religious issue. A good Jews man is not to go into a gentile or Italian household and yet the Spirit of God is leading him to break a barrier and discover something about himself that was inconsistent with

God he said he served. In this instance Peter did not realize that he was in a gentile's house. This is important because we are dealing with a Christian man, born again, and a man who is not only a Christian and born again, but we are dealing with a man in the day of Pentecost when the Spirit of God descended and filled everybody with the Holy Spirit, and all began to speak in other tongues experienced that visitation. We are dealing with a man who actually got up in that caused three thousand people to be born again in a moment. But there is something of concern in Peter's heart and the Holy Spirit had to expose and reveal it. In this moment that is the condition in the church of Jesus Christ and the Holy Spirit is revealing things that may be hidden in the hearts of New Creation believers that they did not even know it was there. He is revealing those things because He is the Spirit of truth. Transformation is always going to occur if you are following Him. Therefore, when Peter goes into the house and begins to preach and in and in his admission it is almost like a disclaim to qualify why he was there. "Acts 10:28 - You know how unlawful it is for a Jewish man to keep company with or go to one of another nation. But God has shown me that I should not call any man common or unclean."

If God had not dealt with Peter, he would not have been in the company of Cornelius and the others with him. If the Spirit of God had not dealt with Peter, his good Christian Spirit-filled soul would not be in this Italian's house. But God dealt with him against his religious attitude. The Spirit of God showed peter that the distinction of his religious traditions had been eradicated by the finished work of Jesus Christ.

It would have been prejudicial and bigoted of him to look at another man of another ethnicity and think that they are different from him because of their traditional upbringing, color, or their ethnicity.

Acts 10:44 says – "While Peter was still speaking these words, the Holy Spirit fell upon all those who heard the word."

Peter did not a chance to finish his sermon or get a chance to play, choir to sing, but the Holy Spirit fell on all those who heard the word. We must understand that Peter's mind is being blown right now because first of all he did not think he was supposed to be there and second the Spirit of God wants Peter to understand what He has accomplished through the blood and the finished work of Jesus, that He does not even let him finish preaching before the people are saved and filled with Holy Spirit.

Acts 10:45 – "And those of the circumcision who believed were astonished, as many as came with Peter, because the gift of the Holy Spirit had been poured out on the Gentiles also."

They were astonished that people who were not of their ethnicity, they were astonished that people they had traditionally been taught to avoid, and they were different from them, and they were astonished that God made no distinction between them. These of circumcision were born again and Spirit-filled people. When they heard Peter had broken a barrier and began to treat people of another ethnicity or persuasion as equal to himself, they contended with him.

In Verse 4-18 Peter had explained why he was dealing with these of uncircumcision, why he was dealing with people of another ethnicity as equal to himself they became silent and glorified God saying, "Then god has also granted to the gentile's repentance to life." In other words, they were saying that if God is saying this then we have to change our minds and our hearts. That is the repentance that God is calling for and challenging the church to adapt. This is not repentance of sin but of dead works, ideologies, mentalities, and perspectives that have been perpetuated and propagated but they are not in line with the scriptures and with the word of God. The word repent doesn't just mean rolling on the floor and being sorry for sin. It means "Again to Think or Think again." The church has erroneously preached that repentance is a change of direction. No! Repentance is first a change of heart and mind that empowers you to change direction. You cannot change direction until you change your heart and mind. The only power that can transform the heart and mind is the gospel of Jesus Nazareth. The most disturbing thing to me as to what is happening with the modern discourse is that the church has no voice in it. The media is not calling on the church to bring a resolve because she failed to live up to the truth of the word of God and has become irrelevant in the discussion. I have to write and help the church to understand the civil rights movement of the 1960s had such great advance because it was fueled by a prophetic mind. Dr. Martin Luther King was not a civil right leader, he was a prophet. His prophetic utterance called the society and the politicians to hear the word of God. When the prophet was struck down the movement fell into the hands of politicians and civil rights leaders, and it stopped having prophetic unction and wind and so it has stalled.

Now the Spirit of the Lord is demanding the church both the so-called black and white to come to the knowledge of the truth and preach it. I am so passionate about this because I am watching my nation kill itself. I am watching an entire generation of young people of African descent stay away from the church altogether because the church has not lived up to on the black-or-white side of the truth of its calling, anointing and grace. God has spoken but who can but prophesy? The Spirit of God is stirring and behind all the protest, social unrest, and all the injustice, and behind all the cries of men and women to get the knees off their necks is the Spirit of God because He is the Spirit of liberty. Whatever liberty is being cried out for; equality is demanded. It doesn't matter whose mouthpiece is, the Spirit of God is behind it. Now the church must take the mantle of its responsibility and interject in the discussion and bring change. This demands that we take a look of Christianity on what it does and does not do. When we look at this text we see Peter, a man that is born again and Spirit filled, but still has remnants and pieces of prejudice in the innerness of his soul and mind. We look at a man who was born again, filled with Spirit and God working with him who still has remnants and recesses of ethnic bias and prejudicial and traditional religious understanding in his heart and in his mind. It takes the spirit of God and a vision to expose it to himself and for him to begin to search himself. This is why David the psalmist in *Psalm 139:23-24 said "search me o God and know my heart, try me and know my thoughts and see if there be any wicked way in me and then lead me in the way everlasting"* because when we examine ourselves whether black or white, we are all white in our own eyes. It is only the Spirit of God can shine the light on human heart and show us where our minds and spirits need to be adjusted. The question that we are to ask ourselves is that what does being born again or being born from above experience do? The presumption that when you are born again and filled with the Holy Spirit all of this is out of you is something that the scriptures don't support. I know this is uncomfortable to many, but I must write out the truth so people can be set free.

We must understand that the born again or born from above experience literally means you must be begotten or born from above. In John 3:5-7 "Jesus answered, "Most assuredly, I say to you, unless one is born of water and the Spirit, he cannot enter the kingdom of God. That which is born of the flesh is flesh, and that which is born of the Spirit is spirit. Do not marvel that I said to you, 'You must be born again'." Nicodemus does not understand some of the things that Jesus was saying, preaching and teaching. To be born again is not simply to get another life, but it is to be born or begotten from the Spirit. Now we must understand this is the key or sublime and seminal event of the Christian life and now as we discuss these things that are confronting us with race, ethnic bigotry, prejudice, social injustice, and inequality we have some understanding of what the born again or born from above experience or event actually is. We must understand what it does and does not do. The born again or born from above experience regenerates the human spirit, it supplants or supersedes or replaces the force of human life with the force of divine life in the spirit and gives the born from above individual to access the fulness of nature, character, and the authority of God. It enables and empowers the individual who is born from above to participate in the transformation of the mind, the will, the emotions, and the physical body by the renewing of the word of the word of God. The born from above experience transforms your spirit, but it doesn't by itself change your mind, will, emotions, and attitudes. You can be born again bigot. Yes, you can be born again and be filled with prejudice because your mind and spirit have been born again, but your mind has not been renewed to the word of God. That is why the bible says in *Romans 12:1-2* "*I beseech you therefore, brethren, by the mercies of God, that you present your bodies a living sacrifice, holy, acceptable to God, which is your reasonable service. 2 And do not be conformed to this world, but be transformed by the renewing of your mind, that you may prove what is that good and acceptable and perfect will of God.*" We must be real with what happens with being born from above. People wonder how there can be prejudice and division in the church! The reason is men's and women's spirits have been reborn, but their minds have not been renewed to the reality of the word of God. The born-from-above experience transforms, regenerates, and empowers it with the very nature, character, and authority of God so that the born-from-above individual can begin to renew their MIND, change their WILL, and control their attitudes by the word of God. God does not do that! You and I must do that and if we fail to recognize the need to do it, we will go on with our lives doing what we normally do thinking God is in favor of it, which indeed He is not. In the above scripture, Paul is speaking to brethren, men, and women of God, to those who have been born from above and not to the world. He is speaking to believers. You and I make the presentation of our bodies a living sacrifice. That means we are alive, but we are sacrificing our WILL, OPINION, and ATTITUDE. The death that Jesus is calling from His followers is not for us to hang on the cross and die like He did. The death of Jesus calling for us is the death of our opinion, attitudes, tradition, religious persuasion, ethnic bias, and our social proclamatory to justice. Reasonable service means true spiritual worship. It means it doesn't matter how much saved one may be until you start making a presentation of yourself to God for transformation you are not worshipping spiritually yet. You are only worshipping in form, structure, and religion. Until you take the word of God with your born-again spirit-filled self and present your mind, will, and emotions to God and say now help me to change this, He says you are not worshipping spiritually yet. This is why the bible says God is looking for men and women who will worship Him in Spirit and truth. He is not talking about jumping, shouting, running around, singing hymns. He is talking about men and women who will worship Him in line with this revelation of the word of God and when their minds, wills, or emotions contradict the word of God they change. They don't expect God to change them, but they change and do not go with the form of the world. Even though you are born again, and Spirit filled, if you do not make the presentation of yourself for transformation you will go with the world's ideas, ideologies, mentalities, and nomenclature rather than enduring the transformation the Spirit of God has called you to because He called us to be conformed into the image of the son. In the final analysis, God has not called us to be ritual prosperity although He will prosper us. He has not called us to be healed although He will heal us. He has not called us to be anything else, but to be conformed to the image of His son and to represent Jesus on the earth. God has called us not to be conformed to this world meaning not to go with the world's form but to allow ourselves to change form. To undergo the change God requires of us for the highest living. The born from above experience empowers the one who has received the light of God into their spirit to begin by the word of God to transform their mind and will because we have thought that God will do it. We think anything we come up with, preach, think, or say after we are born again is acceptable to God. No!

What the born from above experience does not do is significant. The problem is that we assume that the born from above, Spirit filled life itself accomplishes this transformation. This purging of historically infected bigotry or the pulling up of deep-rooted traditional perspectives and bias, we deceive ourselves. If we believe that the born from above experience by itself does the transformation, then we will never truly examine ourselves assuming that we are already completely transformed in these areas when the scripture bears out that we are not. For Peter that transformation required not only a spiritual experience, but it required a social interaction. It was not enough for him to just to know what God was saying but he had to go to the house and preach it and see it experienced. It was not enough for him to be transformed in a corner of a housetop and say I have been changed. No! He had to leave the house and go to Cornelius' house, to actually enter the house of someone that traditionally would not have engaged with and there he sees the power of God.

The ethnic and social discord although I don't believe the term race is applicable and not biblical sometimes you have to utter it in order to expose the lie and bring healing. For ethnic or racial discord in the United States to be healed there must come a new generation of God's people to the table of brotherhood. Dr Martin L King said that one day black and white men would sit down at the table of brotherhood. That is not in Washington DC or Sacramento California, but in the church of the Lord Jesus Christ. The table of brotherhood is where God has made men and women of every ethnicity, brothers by the blood of Jesus. They are diverse, different, culturally different, but one race in Christ Jesus. So, we can begin to dialogue without hatred, jealousy, and bias on a level of equality and then begin to examine our distinctions.

Take a leap of fait before you can see a leap in life. Everything you will ever need is not out there, it is already in you. www.masaalong.com

Social media has seemingly returned to "business as usual," with many brands silent on the social injustices they were so vocal about mere months ago. But remember things: Statements will fade. What will last is the stance that companies, brands, or individuals take.

ABOUT THE AUTHOR

Samuel Davis Kioko, the preacher, accountant, financial analyst, entrepreneur, and author is a native of Kenya and a citizen of The United States of America. He experienced salvation through Jesus Christ at seventeen. Responding to the Holy Spirit's calling, he serves as a missionary, teacher, entrepreneur, and scholar. His ministries connect people to the power of God by preaching and teaching a wholistic gospel to the systems of the world for mankind's whole deliverance. He and his wife Jedidah, a Registered Nurse and preacher, are co-founders of God's big business: KioWanexus Inc. which is a group of companies made up of producing horticulture products, livestock products, real equities, Kinsfolk advocacy, Christian non-fiction-writings-, and, and taking the wholistic gospel to the whole world (world's systems) for mankind's whole deliverance to live victorious lives.

As an author, he has written and published four books–Rejecting Offense Strife and Unforgiveness,

God's Order and Purpose for Marriage, Power Beyond Coronavirus, and Rediscovering the Use of the Tongue. He continues to write and plans to publish more of his books–two manuscripts are ready for publishing:

"Pandemonium Upon Pandemic and "The Ones with Your Assignment." Also, he is near completion of writing two more books – "Increasing in Money Abounding in Love" and "Agents of Restoration."

He trained in business administration (entrepreneurship) and accounting, at California State University. He is also an ordained minister and a member of the Full Gospel Fellowship of Churches and Ministers International (FGFCMI).

In the bucolic landscapes of his youth, Samuel Davis Kioko's journey into the realm of agricultural entrepreneurship unfolded under the watchful guidance of both paternal and maternal grandfathers. Their expertise in livestock and horticulture farming left an indelible mark on Samuel's formative years, igniting a passion that manifested in various endeavors during his off-school days.

Samuel's entrepreneurial spirit sprouted from diverse activities, including crafting artifacts, working as a shepherd boy, and even engaging in the ancient art of wildlife hunting. These pursuits not only showcased his industrious nature but also served as financial stepping stones. Earnings from these ventures were not only used to support his family but also invested in acquiring farm tools, seedlings, and livestock—a testament to his commitment to agricultural aspirations.

However, as Samuel transitioned into high school, geographical distances forced a hiatus on his burgeoning business ventures. Undeterred, his father stepped in, hiring workers to sustain the family's agricultural legacy. Samuel's journey took a transformative turn as he crossed borders, pursuing higher education in the United States with a focus on business administration, accounting, financial management, and computer information systems.

Yet, Samuel's narrative is not merely a chronicle of an Entrepreneurial pursuit. It is a compelling odyssey marked by adversities, including bullying, betrayal, and discrimination. The zenith of these challenges occurred when Samuel, at the tender age of thirteen, stood up for his mother in the face of physical harm, resulting in his estrangement from his father. This poignant episode served as a crucible for Samuel, prompting profound reflections on the omnipresence of hostility in human hearts and the escalating violence within society.

Diving into the complex psychology of anger and forgiveness during his university studies, Samuel discovered a profound truth embedded in biblical wisdom. His exploration unearthed the exorbitant cost of harboring unforgiveness — a theme he passionately addresses in his book, "Rejecting Offense, Strife, and Unforgiveness," adhering to the principles of the Chicago Manual Style.

Grounded in Proverbs 19:11 and Proverbs 10:12, Samuel's work delineates forgiveness as a godlike virtue and its pivotal role in maintaining relationships and preventing societal decay. The book is a roadmap for readers, offering practical advice intertwined with biblical principles and Samuel's personal journey toward liberation through forgiveness.

In the tapestry of Samuel Davis Kioko's life, forgiveness emerges as the linchpin — the force that shattered the shackles of bitterness and opened the door to unbridled freedom. This is not merely a story of Entrepreneurial pursuits; it is an odyssey of resilience, wisdom, and the transformative power of forgiveness — a compelling narrative that transcends time and resonates with readers seeking liberation from the chains of unforgiveness.

www.ingramcontent.com/pod-product-compliance
Lightning Source LLC
Chambersburg PA
CBHW021647120626
46545CB00002B/747